The Story of Lāhainā

Jill Engledow is an award-winning author who specializes in the history of Maui. Her books include *Exploring Historic Upcountry; Island Life 101: A Newcomer's Guide to Hawaiʻi; Haleakalā: A History of the Maui Mountain; The Island Decides,* a novel; and *Sugarcane Days: Remembering Maui's Hawaiian Sugar & Commercial Company.*

This book's cover is from a watercolor by James Gay Sawkins, an English-born artist who visited Hawaiʻi from January 1850 to June 1852. In titling this painting of Waineʻe Church and its surrounding wetlands, Sawkins misidentified the Congregational church—the painting's official name is *The Presbyterian Church, Lahaina.* But he preserved for posterity the now-lost beauty of this lovely section of old Lāhainā and the impressive structure erected by Governor Hoapili and the chiefs of Maui. Visible on the hill above the church is Lāhaināluna Seminary.

In recent decades the renaissance of the Hawaiian language has included the use of two diacritical marks: the ʻokina, or glottal stop, and the kahakō, or macron, which assist with proper pronunciation. This book uses two kahakō in the word Lāhainā, a form followed by the Lāhainā Restoration Foundation and listed in the standard *Place Names of Hawaiʻi* as the "old pronunciation of Lahaina."

The Story of Lāhainā

Jill Engledow

Maui Island Press
Wailuku, Maui, Hawaiʻi

Copyright © 2016 by Jill Engledow

All rights reserved. No part of this book may be reproduced or transmitted in any form or by any means without written permission from the publisher, except for the inclusion of brief quotations in a review.

Cover image by James Gay Sawkins

Designed by Cynthia Conrad
cconraddesign@gmail.com

Published by Maui Island Press
P.O. Box 176
Wailuku, HI 96793-1813

books@mauiislandpress.com
www.mauiislandpress.com

ISBN 978-0-9765136-5-0

Printed in China
10 9 8 7 6 5 4 3 2 1

Names:	Engledow, Jill, author.
Title:	The story of Lāhainā / Jill Engledow.
Description:	Wailuku, Maui, Hawai'i : Maui Island Press, [2016] | Includes index.
Identifiers:	ISBN: 978-0-9765136-5-0
Subjects:	LCSH: Lahaina (Hawaii)--History. | Lahaina (Hawaii)--Pictorial works. | Lahaina (Hawaii)--Guidebooks. | Maui (Hawaii)--History. | Maui (Hawaii)–Guidebooks.
Classification:	LCC: DU629.L33 E54 2016 | DDC: 996.9/21--dc23

CONTENTS

Polynesian Voyagers 1

The *Kapu* Rules 7

Lāhainā Becomes the Kingdom's Capital 17

Christian Converts 22

Lawmaking in Lāhainā 34

The Whaling Era 41

Sugar Brings Workers from Afar 49

Welcoming the World 63

Acknowledgements 75

Index 77

THE STORY OF LĀHAINĀ

INTRODUCTION

More than any place in Hawai'i, the little Maui town of Lāhainā has experienced all the major eras of Island history. In ancient days, Maui chiefs believed to have descended from the gods chose it as their headquarters. Missionaries came to Lāhainā in 1823, bringing Christianity to thousands who gathered to hear their preaching. Whaling ships anchored offshore, resting the crews between arduous journeys to harvest the leviathans of the deep. The third king of the newly united Hawaiian Islands made Lāhainā his capital. Here, the king, the chiefs, and their Western advisors established a system of law that enabled the young kingdom to find its place among the countries of the world. When the whaling industry died out, growers plowed the fields and diverted the streams to establish a sugar plantation, which would bring workers from faraway lands. And, as sugar entered its final half-century as the Islands' economic engine, Lāhainā leaders spearheaded the industry that would replace sugar: tourism.

Today, thousands of travelers from around the world visit the narrow streets of this historic town, reveling in its natural beauty and picturesque architecture. This book is for those among them and everyone else who wonders about the many layers of Hawaiian history and how they interrelate in Lāhainā, a town that has endured and thrived through often-tumultuous centuries.

POLYNESIAN VOYAGERS

The first people to step ashore in Lāhainā must have thought they'd found paradise. Here was a place of stunning beauty that offered everything those pioneers needed to thrive.

Hundreds of years later, the settlement they founded survives—ever changing, but still flourishing on the shores of West Maui.

This place had geographical gifts that promised abundance. The sea was calm, rich with fish and edible seaweeds, and easy to access from a sandy beach. Here, at the foot of the oldest mountains on Maui, time had weathered raw lava into deep soil on a long coastal plain and gently sloping flatlands, perfect for planting.

Artist John Webber documented these sailing canoes greeting Captain James Cook's ships off Hawai'i Island in 1778.
Hawai'i State Archives

Above this fertile land great forests collected rain from clouds clustered around the mountain peaks, sending to the land below streams of that most precious commodity, fresh water. Water is so important to life that the Hawaiian word for wealth—*waiwai*—is simply the word for water—*wai*—repeated twice. Liquid riches flowed in three great streams, Kahoma, Kanahā, and Kauaʻula, and springs of pure water bubbled up to form wetlands and ponds near the shore. Hawaiian farmers built a network of irrigation channels called *ʻauwai*, turning Lāhainā into a garden. The well-watered landscape would someday give this place the nickname "Venice of the Pacific," but from ancient times it has been known primarily by two names: *Lele* and *Lāhainā*.

Lele is the old name for Lāhainā. This word has many meanings. One is "to fly, jump, or leap," a second is "to disembark," as from a canoe, while another is "a detached part of land" belonging to one jurisdiction yet separated from it. Perhaps this name was given because there are many of these small *lele* land divisions near the shoreline here.

Lāhainā, the modern name, can be translated as "cruel sun." One story of its origin tells of a thin-haired chief who cursed the unmerciful

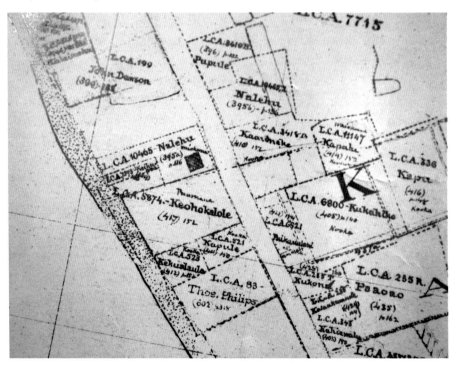

Tiny land divisions made up most of Hawaiian Lāhainā, as recorded on this map from the late 1800s.

sun for burning his uncovered head. Another suggests that the name recalls a terrible drought, when the sun was so fierce that it caused everything to wither and dry.

Besides this town, Lāhainā is the name of a *moku*, a large land division. The Lāhainā Moku stretches from Māʻalaea to Kāʻanapali, one of eleven or twelve *moku* on the island of Maui.

Within each *moku* are land divisions called *ahupuaʻa,* often wedge shaped, many of which extend from the mountaintop to the outer reef, allowing the inhabitants to access the natural resources of the entire area. In Lāhainā, *ahupuaʻa* are unusual in that they often are small and separated from each other, rather than contiguous. Some two dozen *ahupuaʻa* occupy the lands between Launiupoko and Wahikuli.

The chiefs and the commoners considered it their *kuleana*—their responsibility—to live in harmony with nature, managing the resources of their *ahupuaʻa* to ensure that land, water, plants, and sea life were cared for and not overtaxed. For example, fishing of certain species might be prohibited during certain times of year to allow them to breed and multiply, thus protecting the fish supply for the long term. People who lived upstream had *kuleana* regarding their careful use of fresh water, ensuring a supply for those downstream.

The first Polynesian explorers to reach Hawaiʻi brought "canoe crops" like coconut *(niu),* banana *(maiʻa),* sugarcane *(kō),* and taro *(kalo).* This sunny coast with its plentiful water was perfect for a later arrival, breadfruit *(ʻulu),* a beautiful tree producing a starchy, nutritious fruit. An old saying—*Hālau Lāhainā, malu i ka ʻulu*—compares Lāhainā to a large house shaded by breadfruit trees, and the people of ancient Lāhainā spent much of their time

Today, the great breadfruit groves of old times are gone. If you would like to see a beautiful example of the ʻulu, *look behind the Baldwin Home Museum parking lot, where a fine old tree still grows, with deep-lobed leaves and round green fruit ripening to a light-brown color.*

in that luxuriant shade. Another saying, *Lāhainā, i ka malu ʻulu o Lele* (translated by Hawaiian scholar Mary Kawena Pukui as "Lāhainā, in the shade of the breadfruit trees of Lele") is still remembered in the name of a recreational park in the town.

Leeward coasts in Hawaiʻi are hot and dry. Consequently, they were the last areas to be settled, after population growth had filled the more hospitable windward sides, verdant with the moisture of frequent rains. Lāhainā receives only a few inches of rain each year, but it was unique because of its unusual wealth of water from streams and springs. This wealth allowed Lāhainā residents to cultivate *kalo*, a plant that loves water and normally would not thrive on an arid leeward coastline. The *kalo* plant produces an underground corm, or tap root, used to make *poi*.

A contemporary kalo *farmer harvests from his* loʻi. *Both the corm and the leaves, or* lūʻau, *are edible.* Forest and Kim Starr photo

To grow *kalo*, the Polynesian staff of life, early settlers probably planted first along the edges of streams. In time, they would engineer sophisticated irrigation systems to create water-filled fields called *loʻi*, which produced bountiful aquaculture harvests of *kalo*.

For a voyaging people, the channel between their new home and the islands visible from here was not a barrier but a connection. Even other parts of Maui could be reached more easily by canoe than by a rugged trek over the crest of the mountains. Its central location, with easy ocean access to the entire island chain, helped make the Lāhainā Moku a place of power where early chiefs could live and govern not only their own island but those they could see across the ʻAlalākeiki Channel. The islands of Maui, Molokaʻi, Lānaʻi, Kahoʻolawe, and Molokini, together known as Maui Nui—Great Maui—once were under the control of the chiefs of Lāhainā Moku.

Tradition as well as recent archeological study holds that these early settlers lived an easy-going life under the leadership of the headmen of extended families. There are a couple of explanations of how that changed into a more oppressive top-down system dominated by chiefs whose origins were considered divine.

Oral traditions say that in about the thirteenth century a new immigrant arrived who brought a new system. Paʻao may have been from Tahiti or Samoa. After a fight with his brother, he fled north, and landed in Hawaiʻi. Paʻao was displeased to see that previous immigrant chiefs had intermarried with commoners and were not keeping up the rituals of the southern islands. He brought a new chief of unblemished royal blood from the southern islands to establish a new class of *aliʻi* (chiefs) and instituted the rigid system of *kapu* (taboos) that separated the divine *aliʻi* from the common folk. The *kapu* shaped life in Hawaiʻi from that time forward.

Paʻao became the high priest of the *aliʻi* and instituted a strict social, religious, and political hierarchy. He introduced new gods, changed attributes

Aliʻi, *or chiefs, at the pinnacle of ancient Hawaiian society, wore capes and helmets made from thousands of colorful feathers.* Hawaiʻi State Archives

of existing gods to be less peaceful and more bloodthirsty, and built the first *heiau* (place of worship), dedicated to human sacrifice.

Recent scholarship, however, maintains that sometime around A.D. 1500 broader forces—population growth and evolving political relationships—created what would become a more hierarchical society topped by a divine class of *ali'i*.

However they may have attained leadership, the *ali'i* were supported by a growing population and a prosperous agricultural economy. Land management practices and the *Makahiki*, an annual ritual of bringing offerings to the chiefs, focused on maintaining the wealth and power of the *ali'i*. But when population growth outstripped the ability of *kalo* culture to feed the population, these *ali'i* set out to expand their territories, both by growing sweet potatoes in dryland areas and by attacking other *ali'i*. Eventually, consolidated power over an island lay in the hands of a single paramount chief.

When did the Polynesians arrive in Hawai'i?

This is a subject of ongoing debate. For many years, most experts believed the explorers arrived in the first 500 years A.D. Modern carbon dating techniques and other evidence now place the date at around A.D. 1000. Carbon dating of organic materials recovered at Moku'ula, the ancient home of Maui chiefs, has revealed some of the earliest evidence of human habitation in Hawai'i, at approximately A.D. 700.

THE *KAPU* RULES

In old Hawai'i, the *kapu* system defined rights, privileges, restrictions, and responsibilities for all classes of people and managed and preserved natural resources. The *kapu* regulated all of life, from who was in charge to what people could eat and where they could go. Each class had its place in society.

The chiefs, or *ali'i,* administered and managed society and performed rituals to keep the gods, nature, and humanity in balance. Chiefs of the highest rank had the highest levels of mana, or divine power, which made them sacred, and the *kapu* protected them from defilement.

The *kāhuna* were the priestly class, stewards of religious sites and rites. They ensured that everyone obeyed the *kapu*. Along with the *ali'i*, *kāhuna* had the power of life and death over those who broke *kapu*. The *kāhuna* class also included experts who had mastered such arts as canoe making, astronomy, or using plants for medicine.

The common people were called *maka'āinana,* which may be translated "people that attend the land." The Hawaiians of old lived in close harmony with the land, fully aware that they were dependent on its gifts and on each other for survival. The work of the *maka'āinana* was to care for the land that nourished all. And while the *ali'i* were at the peak of the social system, *maka'āinana* were free to leave and find another leader, or even to band together against an oppressive chief, if *ali'i* did not fulfill the responsibilities of their rank to rule for the common good.

Special rules applied to women, who were forbidden some kinds of food—pork, shark's meat, and coconut, for example—except in certain circumstances. Men and women ate separately, with men generally preparing the food for everyone, but eating only with other men. To break this rule was a capital offense. Work also was gender determined.

Men were farmers, fishers, canoe makers; women reared children, made *kapa* (bark-cloth fabric), wove mats and baskets, made nets and cordage.

NĀ ALIʻI—THE CHIEFS

Ancient chants preserve the memories of generations of chiefs who made their homes in Lele, the original name of Lāhainā. The Hawaiians of old measured time by generations and events, not by dates, so we can only estimate when these chiefs lived and ruled. Still, stories of their exploits and adventures remain.

One famous chief, Kakaʻalaneo, ruled jointly with his brother over West Maui and Lānaʻi in the fifteenth century. Renowned for his thrift and energy, Kakaʻalaneo kept court at Kāʻanapali, near the edge of the Lāhainā Moku. He is credited with planting the groves of breadfruit trees for which Lāhainā became famous. Kakaʻalaneo lived near the extinct volcanic cone of Puʻu Kekaʻa (known today as Black Rock), reigning over a land fertile with taro, bananas, sweet potatoes, and breadfruit. When the chief's young son Kaululāʻau mischievously destroyed some

The houses of High Chief Kalanimoku and his wife Likelike are seen in this depiction by Alphonse Pellion, an artist on the Uranie *expedition. Likelike is pounding* kapa *(bark-cloth fabric). Note several Western-style objects in this picture from about 1819: a metal bucket, a table, and doors on the traditional houses.*

of those food plants, his father banished him to the island of Lāna'i across the channel, a place filled with ghosts. The boy managed to kill all the ghosts and became the ruling chief of Lāna'i. Upon his father's death, Kaululā'au became the chief of West Maui and lived once again at Keka'a.

PI'ILANI

Pi'ilani, the grandson of Kaka'alaneo, was ancient Maui's greatest chief and one of the first to be called *mō'ī*, or king, as paramount chief over the entire island. Pi'ilani constructed the West Maui phase of a road that circled the island of Maui. He also rebuilt and expanded Pi'ilanihale, the world's biggest *heiau* (place of worship), in Hāna. Both projects were continued by his son Kiha-a-Pi'ilani.

The Pi'ilani family made their headquarters in Lele. Here was a 17-acre spring-fed freshwater fish pond called Mokuhinia, in which stood a sandbar island known as Moku'ula.

Pi'ilani's daughter, Kalā'aiheana, was born at the birthing stone known as Pōhaku Hauola, still to be seen on the shore near Lāhainā

Lāhainā was quite a different place when its natural waters flowed freely. Here, in 1905, remaining wetlands are a reminder of the glory days, when Mokuhinia was a true pond. Photo courtesy Rob Ratkowski

Harbor. She held the extremely high rank of all her family, reinforced by generations of intermarriage. When she died, she was transformed into one of the many forms of the *moʻo,* or lizard goddess, Kihawahine, and was thereafter referred to as Kihawahine Mokuhinia Kalamaʻula. The *ʻaumakua,* or family god, of the Piʻilani family, Kihawahine guarded them from her grotto under the lake in this *kapu* territory, forbidden to all but the highest *aliʻi.*

Kihawahine's presence was so strong that her power was felt even after the ancient religion was officially overturned. For example, in 1838 the *moʻo* goddess almost capsized Kekāuluohi (*kuhina nui,* or prime minister, from 1839 to 1845), who was going by canoe across the pond of Mokuhinia from Mokuʻula on her way to church at Waineʻe.

———••●●●••———

Piʻilani probably lived on the ocean side of the naturally occurring pond called Mokuhinia. The area is now more frequently referred to as Mokuʻula, the name of the sandbar island which later generations of the Piʻilani family would build up and surround with a retaining wall. In the 1830s and '40s, Kamehameha III used the island as his headquarters. Here is how Western visitor Archibald Menzies described Mokuʻula:

> On our coming near the king's house, the greatest part of them separated from us, particularly the women, on account of the ground around it being tabooed. The royal residence was sheltered with spreading trees and cocoa-nut palms situated near some beautiful fish ponds with which it was more than half surrounded.

The richness of the lands of Lāhainā and those above them is evident from descriptions by early Western visitors. Menzies, who was there in March 1793 in the company of Captain George Vancouver, described traders who visited Vancouver's ship with an "abundance of large gourds, sweet potatoes, watermelons and some musk melons, and plenty of fresh water in calabashes." Along the shore, he noted, were "numerous habitations amongst a grove of cocoanut palms and other trees." Menzies went ashore, climbing with his guides some three miles above the seaside where he observed:

> ... the rugged banks of a large rivulet that came out of the chasm cultivated and watered with great neatness and industry. Even the shelving cliffs of rocks were planted with esculent roots, banked

in and watered by aqueducts from the rivulet with as much art as if their level had been taken by the most ingenious engineer. We could not indeed but admire the laudable ingenuity of these people in cultivating their soil with so much economy.

Menzies described the village of Lāhainā as:

> . . . neatly divided into little fields and laid out in the highest state of cultivation and improvement by being planted in the most regular manner with the different esculent roots and useful vegetables of the country, and watered at pleasure by aqueducts that ran here and there along the banks intersecting the fields, and in this manner branching through the greatest part of the plantation . . . In short, the whole plantation was cultivated with such studious care and artful industry as to occupy our minds and attention with a constant gaze of admiration during a long walk through it.

WARRING CHIEFS

In the 1700s, chiefs of Maui, Oʻahu, and Hawaiʻi Island engaged in a series of wars that led to great destruction of land and people. Warriors destroyed *loʻi kalo* (taro ponds), *loko iʻa* (fish ponds), and complex irrigation systems. Their battles left heaps of human bones and skulls half buried in the sands of Lāhainā Moku. In contrast to the glowing descriptions written by Menzies, his expedition leader, Captain Vancouver, wrote that he found Lāhainā in a "ruinous state" after decades of war.

Maui ruling chief Kahekili and Hawaiʻi chief Kamehameha soon would fight for

Kamehameha was famous for his skills as a warrior, including his ability to snatch thrown spears out of the air. Hawaiʻi State Archives

control of the entire island chain. The elderly Maui chief was on Oʻahu when Kamehameha invaded Maui to beat Kahekili's son in a battle that would win Kamehameha a great prize: a bride of such high status that she was considered divine.

The battle occurred in about 1790, when Kamehameha drove the Maui army from the shores of Central Maui high into Wailuku's ʻĪao Valley. Using Western cannon and muskets for the first time in Hawaiian land battle, the invaders slaughtered the Maui army. The casualties were so great that the battle became known as Kepaniwai, "the damming of the waters," because the bodies of slain warriors blocked the Wailuku River's flow. The victorious Kamehameha claimed the sacred women of the Piʻilani family, including the young girl Keōpūolani. The highest-ranking of Kamehameha's many wives, she would become the mother of three of his children, including the two sons who succeeded him as Kamehameha II and III.

In 1795, after Kahekili died, Kamehameha set out to finally defeat the old chief's son, now residing on Oʻahu, where Kahekili had spent his last days. In preparation for battle, Kamehameha landed a fleet of war canoes at Lāhainā, and his men overran the fields, collecting supplies for an army that might have numbered close to ten thousand. As a strategic by-product, they left the people of Maui struggling to survive and unlikely to rebel against their new leader.

Kamehameha prevailed on Oʻahu, then turned his attention to the island of Kauaʻi. The invasion, in the spring of 1796, ended when wind and waves nearly swamped his fleet. Kamehameha returned to his home island of Hawaiʻi to tamp down a rebellion that had broken out there. Having consolidated his power in the southern islands, he set out once again to take Kauaʻi.

Then, as before, Lāhainā suffered. Kamehameha's army returned to Lāhainā during 1802 and 1803, building a fleet of war canoes for a second attempt at Kauaʻi, again feeding and clothing themselves from the wealth of Maui, Molokaʻi, Lānaʻi, and Kahoʻolawe.

This expedition to Kauaʻi failed even before it left Oʻahu, the final stop before launching an attack. Warriors were struck down by illness (perhaps cholera), one of many diseases that would ravage the population as Western seamen introduced new germs. Kamehameha himself nearly died, and he lost many important chiefs.

Kauaʻi later joined the kingdom of Kamehameha by treaty. For the first time, all the islands of Hawaiʻi were united under one ruler.

The Lāhainā neighborhood where Kamehameha prepared for war was a noble one. Called Luaʻehu, this area had long been home for Maui chiefs and their retainers. Here, Kamehameha built a mud-brick house for his powerful Maui-born wife Kaʻahumanu. It was said to be the first Western-style building constructed in the Hawaiian Islands. Kamehameha repaired the banks of *kalo* fields destroyed in the wars and worked in the royal *loʻi*, Apukaiao, near the "brick palace" by the shore, modeling for his people the value of hard work. He also had his young son, Liholiho, rededicate *heiau* around the island, including two in Lāhainā. Young as he was, the little boy had inherited the sacred *mana* of his mother, Keōpūolani.

HAWAIIANS ASTRIDE

The first horses arrived in Lāhainā in 1803, a gift to King Kamehameha from Captain William Shaler and commercial officer Richard Cleveland of the merchant vessel *Lelia Byrd*. Cleveland had purchased a mare and horse in California, along with a pregnant mare that the ship dropped off at Kawaihae on Hawaiʻi Island. John Young, a former British sailor who had become one of the king's chief advisors, was happy to receive

The Royal Family of Hawaiʻi *by Charles Nahl (engraved by Thomas Armstrong) shows the horse-loving* aliʻi nui *of the mid-19th century, with the ladies wearing* paʻu. *Left to right, Queen Emma, King Kamehameha IV, Princess Victoria, Queen Dowager Kalama, a maid of honor, and Prince Lot Kamehameha.*

an animal he knew could be put to good use. When *Lelia Byrd* arrived in Lāhainā however, Kamehameha was less impressed than Young. The king was busily preparing to invade Kaua'i with a fleet of war canoes, and horses had no place in the Hawaiian style of battle.

Hawaiians eventually would come to love horses and were especially fond of racing, formal or informal. In the late 1800s and early 1900s, Mauians of all classes came to watch and bet on horse races at a track set up on the Kā'anapali shore. The racetrack stretched from the present site of Kā'anapali Beach Hotel to that of the Westin Maui Resort and Spa and provided much excitement, and probably a few tears, until races ended in 1918.

Today, horses can be seen in the annual Kamehameha Day parade down Front Street, decorated with flowers and *lei* and ridden by women wearing the traditional *pa'u*. These lengths of fabric were wrapped to allow the rider to sit astride, rather than sidesaddle, while wearing a long dress. Travel writer Isabella Bird described *pa'u* riders in 1875 as "flying along astride, barefooted, with their orange or scarlet riding dresses streaming on each side beyond their horses' tails, a bright kaleidoscopic flash of bright eyes, white teeth, shiny hair, garlands of flowers." Modern parade *pa'u* riders are more sedate, but just as lovely, atop their flower-adorned steeds.

KEŌPŪOLANI

Keōpūolani, the "sacred wife" of Kamehameha I, was considered sacred because of her high lineage. She was the product of generations of intermarriage between high-ranking *ali'i* of the Pi'ilani line. The marriage of close relatives—full-blood brothers and sisters, half siblings, first cousins—was believed to magnify the *mana,* or power, of the chiefly class, concentrating it so that each succeeding generation was more sacred.

Marriage to Keōpūolani consolidated Kamehameha's new power; his wife was of higher rank than his, and their children would inherit both the divine *mana* of their mother's bloodline and the *mana* their father had achieved through his conquests. Keōpūolani also brought the Pi'ilani family's *mo'o* goddess Kihawahine, whose power helped legitimate and establish Kamehameha's new authority as ruler of the Islands.

Keōpūolani's status was so high that it both protected and restricted her. The near-worship with which she was regarded meant that

Keōpūolani led nothing like a normal life. Most people faced death if they touched or approached her. Even Kamehameha had to remove his *malo* (loincloth) in her presence and crawl to approach her. Keōpūolani seems to have been a kind woman who did her best to protect others from her powerful *kapu,* so that no one was put to death because of it. She remained close to her sons, who were handed over, as tradition required, to be raised by other *ali'i,* but insisted on keeping daughter Nāhi'ena'ena with her.

KAMEHAMEHA

Kamehameha, called "The Great" because he united the Island chain, was a strong king and able ruler. Born in North Kohala on Hawai'i Island, he was not of the highest rank but was close to power, the nephew of the ruling chief, Kalaniopu'u. Kamehameha was a formidable warrior, famous for such feats as catching spears tossed by opponents while training for battle. The young chief also caught a glimpse of astounding new ways and weapons aboard the ship of Captain James Cook, the British explorer whose 1778 visit was the first contact of Hawai'i with the Western world.

Kamehameha I

When Kalaniopu'u died, he left his son Kīwalaō as his successor and gave Kamehameha the guardianship of the war god. Soon, civil war wracked the island; Kamehameha first defeated Kīwalaō, then killed his brother Keōua. Kamehameha now dominated Hawai'i Island and was able to focus on fighting Kahekili, king of Maui. His defeat of Kahekili's son after the old chief's death gave him control of every island but Kaua'i and its neighbor, Ni'ihau. Their chief ceded them peacefully to Kamehameha in 1810 and continued to rule his islands as part of the new kingdom.

After years of civil war, Kamehameha worked to restore the ravaged lands and produce food for the hard-pressed population. He also wove a careful path through the major changes descending on his kingdom as more and more foreigners arrived. A canny businessman, he skillfully developed the sandalwood trade, which brought great revenues to the kingdom. He selectively incorporated foreign technologies and skills, surrounding himself with supportive newcomers, as well as his reliable *ali'i* advisors. And he was a conservative who strictly maintained the ancient religion despite the damage of foreign ideas undermining Hawaiian values.

Kamehameha made his final court in Kailua-Kona on Hawai'i Island. There he died in 1819, leaving his kingdom to his son Liholiho in a time of increasing change. Queen Ka'ahumanu stepped forward to take a new position, *kuhina nui*—regent or prime minister.

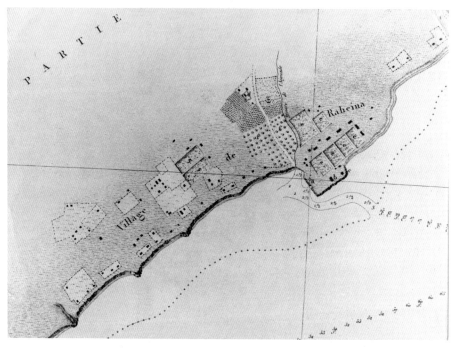

The "point" of Lāhainā in 1819, drawn during a visit by the French ship Uranie *under Captain Louis de Freycinet. Letters in this first map ever drawn of Lāhainā identify various objects: the* Uranie's *observatory, for calculating longitude and latitude, the Brick House, and a "morai," their spelling of the Tahitian word for* heiau. *The larger rectangles are* lo'i kalo *(ponds for growing taro), and the stream that would become Dickenson Street runs beside plantations of sugarcane and the paper mulberry, from which* kapa *is made.* Hawai'i State Archives

LĀHAINĀ BECOMES THE KINGDOM'S CAPITAL

Soon after the death of Kamehameha I, Queens Keōpūolani and Ka'ahumanu cooperated with High Priest Hewahewa to overthrow the *kapu* system, which had governed life in Hawai'i for many generations. Perhaps it was clear to them, as to other Hawaiians, that the Western newcomers were able to ignore the system's strict rules without consequence. A new way of life was intruding upon the Islands, and it had irretrievably damaged the ancient social system.

Keōpūolani and Ka'ahumanu coerced the new king, Liholiho, to share a meal with them, thus breaking a key *kapu* forbidding men and women to eat together. This pivotal event effectively overthrew their ancestral religion. Not all Hawaiians agreed—there was a brief revolt, and many customs and rituals went underground. But around the Islands, temple gods were burned, *heiau* destroyed, and the old system came tumbling down. A few months later, Christian missionaries arrived from the United States, finding to their surprise that the great old king had died and the *kapu* system was gone. Keōpūolani, who had given up her own uniquely high (and perhaps burdensome) *kapu* status by overturning the system that supported it, began to study this new religion.

Kamehameha II

Liholiho was a restless king, moving from island to island, but his siblings, Kauikeaouli and Nāhiʻenaʻena, set up households in Lāhainā. In May 1823 they were joined by their mother, Keōpūolani, with her new husband, Hoapili, who became governor of Maui. Other chiefs accompanied the revered queen to the old home of the Piʻilani line. Keōpūolani also brought with her the missionaries Charles and Harriet Stewart and William and Clarissa Richards, an African-American teacher named Betsey Stockton who accompanied the Stewarts, and a Tahitian Christian named Tauʻa. They would introduce the Gospel to Maui.

A grass house near the shore occupied by Nāhiʻenaʻena and later by a Lāhainā merchant.

Keōpūolani and other chiefs lived on the land that today is the site of Kamehameha III Elementary School. Nearby were large *kalo* fields, on the point of land fronting the harbor that now is shaded by an enormous banyan tree and the site of the Pioneer Inn, the Old Lāhainā Courthouse, and the public library. The queen's newfound interest in Christianity and support of the missionaries began to influence the formerly high-living *aliʻi*, leading them to worship the Christian God and to take up reading and writing.

But the queen was in her last year of life. She died September 16, 1823, shortly after being baptized and becoming the first official Hawaiian convert to Christianity. The much-loved queen's death was

Young ali'i *Kauikeaouli and Nāhi'en'ena posed for Robert Dampier in 1825. The English artist arrived aboard the ship that returned the bodies of Kamehameha II and his queen from England, so Kauikeaouli was officially king at this time, though Ka'ahumanu retained power. Dampier painted the young royals in oil, covering the Western silks they preferred with traditional feather capes. These engravings are taken from the original oil paintings.*
Hawai'i State Archives

marked by the gathering of hundreds to wail in grief. But, as she had commanded, there was no wild mourning in the traditional ways that ranged from half-shaved heads to self-inflicted burns to the death of a chief's retainers. She was the first *ali'i* to be buried Western style, in a tomb built of stone.

The queen's death drew many prominent *ali'i* to Lāhainā, where they stayed for some time following her funeral. While on Maui, Liholiho informed a council of the chiefs that he wanted to visit England. He named his younger brother Kauikeaouli as his successor in case he did not return. In the end, he did not; both the king and his wife died of measles in London. The eleven-year-old Kauikeaouli was now Kamehameha III.

The young monarch's reign would be controlled at first by *Kuhina Nui* Ka'ahumanu, who enacted strict laws influenced by her conversion to Christianity. After her death, in 1832, the young king rebelled and returned to traditional ways. This included an intimate relationship with his beloved sister Nāhi'ena'ena.

By ancient custom, the two had been brought up to mate in order to concentrate the *mana* of children they might bear. Despite the pleas of missionaries, who had great influence over her, Nāhiʻenaʻena became pregnant, perhaps with her brother's child, perhaps with the child of the young chief to whom she was officially married. Born prematurely in late 1836, the child died, and Nāhiʻenaʻena died soon after.

Grief stricken, Kauikeaouli retreated to Mokuʻula, the island in the sacred pond, and built a tomb for her, her child, and Keōpūolani. Kauikeaouli would spend nearly a decade at this place, the home of his ancestral guardian Kihawahine and longtime center of *aliʻi* power. He lived a traditional lifestyle in a grass house on Mokuʻula, while an unfinished palace near the beach, Hale Piula, served as a place to meet with occasional foreign visitors. Access to the sacred island was strictly controlled; here, the king could live the life he chose without interference from missionaries. They were nearby, but could not visit the island without the king's invitation. He did not invite them.

But the king's residence at his ancestral home was not to last. The world was intruding, and though Kauikeaouli left much of the kingdom's business to his *kuhina nui* in Honolulu, international relationships increasingly required the king's attention. In 1845, the court moved to Honolulu. The excellent harbor there attracted ships from foreign lands, along with the newcomers who continued to bring the ways of the Western world, and many of its troubles.

Honolulu, 1854, by artist Paul Emmert

HOAPILI

High Chief Hoapili, governor of Maui for nearly two decades, was a leader of the kingdom, the island of Maui, and the town of Lāhainā through the difficult years of transition from the autocracy of Kamehameha I to the constitutional monarchy of his son, Kamehameha III. Born Ulumaheihei, he was given the name Hoapili (close friend) by Kamehameha I, to whom he was a trusted advisor.

The dying Kamehameha I chose Hoapili and his brother to hide his bones (potent with the king's *mana*) in a secret cave and charged Hoapili with the care of Queen Keōpūolani. The pair married after the king's death. They moved to Lāhainā, where Christianity took root and where the chiefs enacted laws that Hoapili enforced strictly but fairly. Hoapili led the building of the island's first stone church, at Waine'e, and erected a fort at the harbor to guard the village against foreign ships and lawbreakers. His ban on liquor in Lahaina, from 1824 to 1840, was one reason whaling-ship captains favored Lāhainā Roads. Temperance made for more easily controlled crews ashore and a more peaceful port. Hoapili helped raise several royal children and is remembered as a strong and able governor.

CHRISTIAN CONVERTS

Calvinist missionaries who arrived in the Islands in 1820 were greeted with news of the recent death of Kamehameha I and the astonishing overthrow of the native religion by his successors. These events followed nearly forty years of foreign contact that already had disrupted a centuries-old tradition, religion, and economy. The missionaries found a people open to new learning and spiritual ideas and in need of education to help them cope with an increasingly intrusive outside world. These New England Protestants brought with them the unconscious ethnocentrism of their time, imposing their Puritan values on a people and a culture they did not understand. Their preaching, accepted and enforced by the *ali'i,* drove much of Hawaiian culture underground. But they also brought the essential power of *palapala*—literacy—a power Hawaiians needed in this new world.

For several decades after Keōpūolani brought the first missionaries to Lāhainā in 1823, they and their successors would provide important services to the people of Lāhainā, with minimal support from the American Board of Commissioners for Foreign Missions in New England as they helped the people and their chiefs through a difficult time of transition. The first missionaries to Hawai'i had devised an alphabet for the oral Hawaiian language, and the Hawaiians were so eager to learn that by the mid-1800s Hawai'i was one of the most literate nations in the world. *He aupuni palapala ko'u,* said Kauikeaouli, Kamehameha III: Mine is a kingdom of literacy.

The newly literate Hawaiians set about preserving their ancient chants and stories in books and dozens of Hawaiian-language newspapers, leaving an invaluable legacy for generations to come. Though the Hawaiian language was no longer used in public schools after the late 1800s, and it neared extinction in the twentieth century, much of its oral history and poetic language already had been preserved in hundreds of thousands of printed pages. In the twenty-first century, as Hawaiian education revives the language and wisdom of ancient days, these writings are a rich source of history and inspiration.

LĀHAINĀ MISSIONARIES

Missionaries Charles Stewart and William Richards, who arrived with Queen Keōpūolani, introduced Christianity to the people of Lāhainā and instructed the chiefs in reading, writing, and religion. The queen generously provided for their needs, giving them land near her own residence and the royal *kalo* fields.

The Stewarts left after three years, due to Mrs. Stewart's health, and their companion, Betsey Stockton (who had established the first reading classes for commoners) went with them.

The Richards family remained, and William Richards played a key role in the mission work and the development of the kingdom. He helped to translate the Bible, was the first pastor of Waineʻe Church (now called Waiola), and helped found Lāhaināluna Seminary. In 1838, he left the mission to work for the kingdom, serving in several important jobs before his death in 1846. He is buried in Waineʻe Cemetery.

Perhaps the best-known of all the missionaries who served in Lāhainā were the Baldwins. Dr. Dwight Baldwin and his wife, Charlotte, arrived in Lāhainā in 1835, assigned to Waineʻe Church when the Richards

Dr. Dwight Baldwin and Charlotte Fowler Baldwin   Hawaiian Mission Houses

family traveled to the United States to enroll their children in schools there. The Baldwins moved into a house built by Dwight's predecessor, the Reverend Ephraim Spaulding, on land set back from the shoreline. As their family grew and they hosted a range of visitors, they added rooms and eventually a second story. The house still stands, prominent on Lāhainā's Front Street. The oldest Western structure on Maui, it is now the Baldwin Home Museum.

Trained as a physician, Dr. Baldwin had been caught up in religious fervor that swept New England, sending missionaries out into the world. At age thirty-two, he was accepted for the mission to Hawai'i before he was able to finish his medical degree. With a newlywed wife, Charlotte, Baldwin left for Hawai'i armed instead with a Master of Science degree, officially ordained to spread the Gospel and equipped with enough medical knowledge that he was able to offer help to Hawaiians facing frightening new diseases like whooping cough and measles, dysentery and influenza. Baldwin worked relentlessly for thirty-three years, traveling to Lāna'i and Moloka'i by canoe and whaleboat, riding horseback to visit patients in Hāna. Besides his medical work,

The Baldwin home played host to many a visitor.
Photo courtesy Rob Ratkowski

he pastored Waineʻe Church, ministered to its members and to the seamen who visited the town, superintended the schools, and handled the business of the Lāhainā mission.

Baldwin is credited with limiting the spread of smallpox in the 1853 epidemic, getting Lāhainā quarantined and its residents vaccinated, and then setting out to care for people around the island. While thousands of people died on Oʻahu, Baldwin reported that only two Lāhainā residents died, along with six who arrived in Lāhainā already sick. In 1855, the congregation of Waineʻe Church built Hale Aloha in gratitude for having escaped the smallpox epidemic. The building was used as a school, meeting place, and parish hall for many years.

Waineʻe Church.
Detail from James Gay Sawkins painting.

As the sponsoring mission society in the United States withdrew financial support, Baldwin and other missionaries who wanted to stay in the Islands were forced to fend for themselves. This resulted in some of them and their children going into business. One of Dr. Baldwin's sons, Henry P. Baldwin, joined Samuel T. Alexander (son of William P. Alexander, head of Lāhaināluna Seminary) to found Alexander & Baldwin, a sugar company that would become one of the Islands' biggest corporations.

WOMEN OF THE MISSION

Fired by their desire to share their Christian faith, the female missionaries of the American Board of Commissioners for Foreign Missions for the Sandwich Islands abandoned all they had known in New England to live in a far-off foreign land. To meet the board's usual requirement that missionaries be married, some were newly wed to men they had just met.

Once in Hawaiʻi, however, their evangelical fervor had to find a way of fitting in around a nineteenth-century housewife's many chores and duties, multiplied by the never-ending flow of guests who gathered at their tables. After a five-month sea journey around Cape Horn, these young missionaries often found themselves already pregnant with the first of many babies. In the early days, they kept house, gave birth, and reared children in grass houses with dirt floors.

When a violent storm pounded their seaside hut, Harriet Stewart sat for hours clutching her baby, "watching the motion of the rafters in the contentions of the wind—ready to make an escape with him from the ruins of our cabin," husband Charles wrote.

A few years later, Clarissa Richards hid in the cellar as five cannon shots landed near their house, fired by sailors who blamed her husband for High Chief Hoapili's demand that Hawaiian women on their ship be returned to shore.

For more than three decades, Charlotte Fowler Baldwin played hostess to as many as twenty guests on any given day, from whaling-ship captains and their families to visiting scientists, despite her ongoing asthma attacks. She bore eight children, but lost two little ones before their third birthdays.

The cares and labor that filled the days of these and other Lāhainā missionary women surely distracted them and probably exhausted them. But it did not dim their zeal to teach and evangelize. In between supporting husbands in their own multifaceted jobs, making the families' clothes, and chiseling hardened flour from a barrel drenched in saltwater on the journey from New England, they managed to fit in prayer sessions, hymn singing, and Bible study. They taught subjects from sewing classes to geography to both their congregations and their own offspring.

And then, when those children needed higher education, their mothers waved farewell as the young ones sailed away to Honolulu or even New England.

BETSEY STOCKTON

Betsey Stockton

Betsey Stockton, born a slave in New Jersey about 1798, brought the gift of literacy to the common people of Maui. She was the first single woman and the only black missionary to be part of the Sandwich Islands Mission. Betsey had belonged to a family who encouraged her learning and eventually freed her. She arrived in Hawai'i with family friends Charles and Harriet Stewart, sailing to Lāhainā with them in 1823, along with Harriet's infant son she had helped deliver aboard their ship from New England.

Stockton's contract with the mission board called for her to be treated "neither as an equal nor as a servant, but as a humble Christian friend." In addition to assisting the Stewarts, she would participate in the mission's work. In Lāhainā, she was asked to teach reading and began her first class with four English and six Hawaiian students. This was to be the beginning of teaching commoners, rather than only the *ali'i*.

Stockton's time in Hawai'i was short, as Mrs. Stewart's health deteriorated after her second child was born. Before leaving with the Stewarts in 1825, she trained native teachers to take over her work. Stockton maintained her friendship with the Stewart family, and worked as a teacher in Canada, Princeton, and Pennsylvania. The work this "humble Christian" did in Hawai'i contributed to the high level of literacy that would become common among the people.

A Lost Population

It's hard to imagine the ongoing tragedy experienced by the Hawaiian community in the first century after Western contact. No one knows how many people lived in the Islands at the time of contact, but epidemics of diseases like cholera, measles, smallpox, and whooping cough brought by foreign ships had wiped out an estimated 90 percent of the population by the end of the reign of Kamehameha III.

Some fifty-three years after foreign diseases arrived with Captain Cook, the first census conducted by missionaries in 1831 counted 8,415 residents in the district of Lāhainā. At the next census, in 1835, the count was 5,234. By 1866, it was only 3,581. Many who survived the plagues that swept through the Islands were infected with venereal diseases that rendered them infertile, further devastating a Native Hawaiian population already suffering great loss.

WAINE'E CHURCH

Maui's oldest church has been through many changes since its founding in 1823. The landscape around Waiola Church is nothing like the stream-fed wetland of its early days, and the structure itself has been rebuilt several times.

The first grass church, in the area now known as Campbell Park, offered services within weeks of the arrival of Christian missionaries. On September 14, 1828, workers under the leadership of High Chief Hoapili laid a cornerstone for a more permanent building near the site of the present church on Waine'e Street, and the new structure was dedicated in March 1832. The first stone church in Hawai'i, it was two stories high and seated three thousand people. On dedication day, the congregation overflowed to the grounds outside. The church at first was called Ebenezera (Ebenezer), but later became known as Waine'e (moving water) Church.

In 1858, half the roof and the steeple were destroyed by the Kaua'ula wind, a famously destructive wind that sweeps down from Kaua'ula Valley. The church was rebuilt and rededicated. But in 1894 it was destroyed when a burning ember from a rubbish fire landed on the roof. In April 1897, a smaller church was dedicated; with the decreasing population and more denominations offering services in Lāhainā, the congregation had shrunk. This building was paid for by sugar magnate Henry P. Baldwin to honor his father, Dr. Dwight Baldwin, the church's pastor from 1837 to 1868.

Waiola Church today

The church was destroyed yet again by embers from another rubbish fire in 1947. A new building, dedicated the following spring, lasted until January 1951, when it too was destroyed by the Kaua'ula wind. Rebuilt once more and dedicated in April 1953, the church was renamed Waiola Church—living water. It remains in service today, with a congregation that cherishes its historic past and cemetery, where lie the remains of pioneering missionaries and early Hawaiian Christians.

LĀHAINĀLUNA

For nearly two centuries, Lāhaināluna has been one of the most important institutions in Lāhainā. The Lāhainā community and thousands of alumni take great pride in this school, the oldest secondary school west of the Mississippi. The school's motto comes from David Malo, a member of the first class who enrolled at age thirty-eight and went on to become a famous scholar: *O kēia ke kukui pio ʻole i ka makani o Kauaʻula,* it reads: This is the torch never extinguished by the winds of Kauaʻula.

The American Board of Commissioners for Foreign Missions established Lāhaināluna Seminary in 1831 on land given by Chiefess Kalakua Hoapiliwahine, wife of Governor Hoapili. The name Lāhaināluna means "above Lāhainā," and the school looks down over spectacular scenery, with the shoreline, the ocean, and the islands of Lānaʻi and Molokaʻi on the horizon.

Lāhaināluna Seminary was set in the hills luna *(above)* Lāhainā.

Here, Hawaiian men lived alongside their instructors while they learned to read and write in preparation for lives as teachers, ministers, and government officials. Many of the students of its early years went on to become important citizens of the kingdom. The seminary's classes were conducted in Hawaiian, and the school's founder, the Reverend Lorrin Andrews, translated some fifteen books to be used as texts.

Hale Pa'i, the printing house, is now a small museum. This photo was taken before its restoration. Library of Congress, HABS HI, 5-LAHA, 11-1

He also authored the first Hawaiian dictionary and the first Hawaiian grammar book.

Missionary headquarters in Honolulu sent over a printing press in 1834. Andrews had a limited amount of experience with printing, but he helped the students learn how to set type, operate the old press, create copper engravings, and bind books. Three years later, the school built Hale Pa'i, a printing house where the seminary students produced the first newspaper west of the Rockies (called *Ka Lama,* The Torch) and the first paper money printed in the Islands, along with maps, textbooks, and collections of writing about Hawaiian history and culture.

In 1849, Lāhaināluna transferred from mission control to become a public institution of higher learning. In 1903, it became a vocational trade school and in 1923, a public technical high school, admitting both girls and boys as day students. The school has provided a boarding program for boys since 1836, admitting girls as boarders in 1980. The boarding program has an agricultural emphasis. Boarders work on the school farm and around the campus.

Boarders also maintain the L, a stone emblem high above the school on the round slopes of Puʻu Paʻupaʻu, near the grave of David Malo. Twice a year, boarders hike up to the L to clean the area and whiten the symbol with lime. At graduation time, as the senior boarders chorus sings at the commencement ceremony below, alumni light flares around the L, and the torch of learning illuminates the night sky.

DAVID MALO

One of the best-remembered Hawaiians of his time and the source of much information about life in the days before Western contact, David Malo was born in North Kona, on Hawaiʻi Island, in 1795. His father belonged to the court of Kamehameha, and young Malo grew up in the household of the high chief Kuakini, a brother of Kamehameha's queen Kaʻahumanu. Steeped in the old traditions and religious ceremonies of the *kapu* system, Malo came to be regarded as a great authority on Hawaiian lore.

David Malo warned of overwhelming Western influence.

Arriving in Lāhainā the same year as the missionaries, 1823, Malo became a student of the Reverend William Richards and converted to Christianity, receiving the baptismal name of David. An avid scholar, Malo devoured all the learning he could. He helped translate books from the Bible so they could be published in the Hawaiian language and, along with other Lāhaināluna scholars, began writing about Hawaiian religion and cultural history. His book *Moʻolelo Hawaiʻi, or Hawaiian Antiquities,* became an important resource for future students of Hawaiian culture.

Not only a man of books, Malo grew cotton and had cloth woven and made into a suit, which he wore to demonstrate a possible industry for the Islands. He also experimented with growing sugarcane and making sugar and molasses. Dr. Dwight Baldwin, who helped him sell his molasses to the Honolulu mission station, wrote of Malo that he had "perhaps the strongest mind of any man in the nation." Appointed general school agent for the island of Maui in 1841, he later became the first superintendent of schools for the kingdom. He was elected as representative from Maui to the kingdom's first House of Representatives.

In 1848, Malo went to live in Ukumehame and preach in its church. Four years later, he left his Ukumehame posting to serve the people of Kula District in Keokea and Kīhei, founding churches whose walls still stand. He died in Kīhei in 1853. He is buried near the L on the hill above his alma mater, Lāhaināluna, in compliance with his wish to be buried beyond the rising tide of foreign influence he predicted would overwhelm the people of Hawai‘i.

Lāhaināluna High School honored its famous graduate by naming its boys' dorm after him and celebrates his legacy with the annual David Malo Day.

———•●●●••———

If a big wave comes in large fishes will come from the dark ocean which you never saw before, and when they see the small fishes they will eat them up; such also is the case with large animals, they will prey on the smaller ones; the ships of the white men have come, and smart people have arrived from the Great Countries which you have never seen before, they know our people are few in number and living in a small country; they will eat us up, such has always been the case with large countries, the small ones have been gobbled up.
—David Malo, 1837

———•●●●••———

CATHOLIC MISSIONARIES

The first Roman Catholic missionaries were met with suspicion by Hawai‘i leaders, who were loyal to the Protestant missionaries and the variety of Christianity they had introduced. The government subjected native Catholic converts to punishment and expelled Catholic priests, most of whom were members of the French Order of the Sacred Hearts of Jesus and Mary. Still, the priests who were able to spend any time in Hawai‘i managed to share their message, and more Hawaiians were attracted to Catholicism.

King Kamehameha III issued an ordinance in 1837 forbidding the teaching or practice of Catholicism in the kingdom. Two years later, responding to advice from some Protestant missionaries and sea captains, and fearing French reprisals, the king ordered that native Catholics should no longer be persecuted. Gradually, Catholic missionaries resumed their work; in years to come, the king's "Edict of Toleration" would keep the door open for other religions, including Episcopalians, Mormons, Methodists, and other Christian denominations, and immigrant workers from Asia would establish thriving Buddhist and Shinto communities.

The first Catholic Mass on Maui was celebrated in 1841 by pioneer Hawai'i priest Father Louis Maigret on the shore a few hundred yards south of Hale Piula. The property was owned by Joaquin Armas, a Mexican cowboy who was the "king's bullock catcher," in charge of rounding up wild cattle that roamed the island.

Enthusiastic converts had been busy spreading the word on Maui, so there was a ready audience when a contingent of priests arrived from France in 1846. They established themselves in Lāhainā, which became known as the "Cradle of the Faith" on Maui, and sent missionary priests traveling around the island. The Lāhainā church, named Maria Lanakila (Our Lady of Victory), met at first in adobe and grass houses. The priests also set up a small one-classroom school.

This plaque marks the site of the first Catholic Mass celebrated on Maui.

Officially dedicated in 1858, the church was rebuilt with stone in 1873, and that structure still stands, the original Catholic church of Maui. The adjacent cemetery headstones and memorials hold the names of many early Maui Catholic families and of seamen who perished far from home.

In 1941, Lāhainā Catholics dedicated a plaque near Armas' former property to commemorate the first Mass on Maui. The plaque still can be seen on a stone wall along the residential area at the southern end of Front Street.

LAW MAKING IN LĀHAINĀ

Over the years, Lāhainā was the site of several important steps in the evolution of a new style of government for the Hawaiian Islands. Kamehameha the Great had been a strong ruler in complete control of his kingdom. His sons were young and weak, and the kingdom was increasingly challenged by outsiders and by the worldly customs they brought, tempting the Hawaiian people with liquor and imported material goods. The chiefs began to play a larger role in what had been an autocracy. With the king and *kuhina nui,* they struggled to establish a new system to replace the one they had discarded with the overthrow of the *kapu* system.

Hale Paʻahao (stuck-in-irons house) was built in the early 1850s to house whalers and others who got too rowdy. The heavy coral blocks in its walls were taken from the old fort near the harbor, now partially reconstructed.
Library of Congress, HABS HI, 5-LAHA, 4-1

The chiefs who were most influenced by the missionaries thought that the Ten Commandments might be a good set of laws to adopt, and an 1823 proclamation ordered strict observance of the Sabbath. In Lāhainā in 1824, Kaʻahumanu proclaimed a simple code of laws, forbidding murder, theft, boxing or fighting, work or play on the Sabbath, and requiring that "when schools are established, all people shall learn the *palapala*."

Some foreigners wanted the freedom to continue the rowdy lifestyle they enjoyed, but the chiefs set out to suppress vice such as drunkenness, adultery, and gambling. This enraged visiting sailors, who spent their spring and autumn breaks from whaling in pursuit of rum and women. Though the chiefs made the laws, the whalers blamed the church, and between 1825 and 1827 engaged in scuffles with Lāhainā missionaries.

King Kamehameha III enacted laws against murder, theft, and adultery, and told his people three more were on the way, forbidding rum selling, prostitution, and gambling. As more foreigners arrived, intent on doing business, the king and his chiefs were forced to consider lawmaking that went beyond rules about personal behavior. Foreigners wanted to reside in Hawai'i while relying on their own governments' laws and power to protect them. They also wanted control of the land where they established businesses, yet Hawaiian custom was for a chief to grant use of land only until he or she wanted it back. In the end, all land belonged to the king.

When conflicts with foreigners arose, great powers sent warships whose captains insisted that the Hawaiian government concede to demands of the foreign residents. Even friendly ship captains advised the Hawaiian leaders to adopt policies more in line with those of other nations. The outside world encroached, and the kingdom's rulers lacked the skills and knowledge they needed to protect their Islands. The chiefs asked Lāhainā missionary William Richards, who was traveling to the United States, to find an advisor to help the king and chiefs deal with these unprecedented demands. Unable to find such a counselor, Richards gave in to the urgent request that he take the job. He left the mission and began a course of instruction for the chiefs on politics, economics, and government.

William Richards

By 1839, power was divided among the king, the *kuhina nui,* and the informal council of chiefs. In that year, Lāhaināluna Seminary students worked with Richards, the king, and the chiefs to create a declaration of rights sometimes called the Hawaiian

Magna Carta. This defined and secured the rights of the people and addressed issues of taxes, inheritance, and fishing and water rights. For the first time, one could leave two-thirds of one's property to an heir, with only one-third reverting to the king in the customary manner.

In the late 1830s, the chiefs of the Hawaiian Kingdom sat in their ancient capital, not far from the sacred pond at Mokuhinia, meeting in a traditional longhouse as they deliberated their country's future. From their work, based on concepts of government William Richards had explained, came the Constitution of 1840, in which they gave up their chiefly absolute authority to establish the rule of law. This surrender of power was, says one student of the period, a "great act of generosity."

Lāhainā as seen from the hills above town in 1854.

In October 1840, the king and *kuhina nui* signed the constitution. It was called the Lua'ehu Constitution, because it was written and signed in the Lua'ehu neighborhood of Lāhainā, in the traditional longhouse, about where today's public library is located. This constitution created a House of Representatives to be chosen by the people, for the first time giving the common people a share in the government. The other half of the new legislative body—the council of chiefs, with the king and *kuhina nui*—would come to be called the House of Nobles. The kingdom was now a constitutional monarchy, with freedom of religion, the right to a fair trial, and laws regarding taxation.

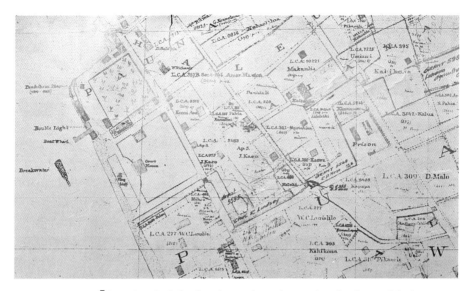

The Māhele ʻĀina *divided the land into lots that individuals could claim. In this map, notice the ancient royal* loʻi kalo *on the "point of Lāhainā," where the public library now stands; the courthouse built in 1865; and numerous lots marked by the letters L.C.A., standing for Land Commission Award.*
Lāhainā Restoration Foundation

THE MĀHELE ʻĀINA

Outside the kingdom, the great European political powers prowled the Pacific, seeking territory to devour. From their point of view, any piece of land not "owned" in a way they understood was available for them to claim. In Hawaiʻi, land and resources traditionally were controlled by the highest chiefs, who authorized their representatives *(konohiki)* to allow commoners *(makaʻāinana)* the use of smaller pieces. No one "owned" land in the Western sense, except perhaps the king.

Tiny and vulnerable, Hawaiʻi several times had to give in to foreigners in conflicts over the use of land because sea captains backed up their countrymen with warships. *Haole* (foreign) residents and subjects of the kingdom also objected to the traditional land ownership pattern because they were hesitant to enter into business deals on land they did not own.

The king's advisors had by 1845 persuaded him that the best solution to these problems was to institute a system of private property ownership. The resulting land division—the *Māhele ʻĀina*—split the land among the king, the government, and the chiefs. In 1849, the Kuleana Act allowed tenants to apply to a land commission and claim fee-simple ownership of their small lots within those larger categories.

The work of the commission was complete by 1855, and anyone who had not laid claim to the land where they lived and grew their crops had lost the right to apply for fee-simple ownership. In the end, the *Māhele* gave the king not quite a million acres, the chiefs and the government each about 1.5 million acres, and the common people less than 30,000 acres.

While the intention had been for *maka'āinana* to acquire their own small plots of cultivated land, or *kuleana,* relatively few people managed to stake their claim in the complicated and confusing division of lands, and some who did later traded land for cash. As a result, many people who already had suffered losses now became landless peasants in their own kingdom. Foreigners, on the other hand, understood well the value of land ownership, and they acquired property, often in large tracts, where they began to plant crops they hoped would earn cash.

KAUIKEAOULI

Kamehameha I brought the islands together, creating the Kingdom of Hawai'i, but it fell to his son Kauikeaouli to maintain that kingdom and connect it to the rest of the world. Reigning as Kamehameha III after the death of his brother, he was the longest ruling of any Hawaiian sovereign, 1825 to 1854. Kauikeaouli was a child when he inherited the throne, and his path to adulthood and control of his kingdom was neither straight nor simple. Yet he managed to balance the demands of tradition and modernity, the needs of his people and the influence of outsiders.

Kauikeaouli, Kamehameha III, as a young man. Hawai'i State Archives

Like his sister Nāhi'ena'ena, Kauikeaouli spent his early years pressured by missionaries and Christian chiefs to reject the ancient pleasures and privileges of the *ali'i.* He enjoyed those royal rights too much to give in to this pressure and chose to maintain relationships the missionaries found sinful and to drink, dance, and play cards, often with the encouragement of foreigners who opposed the missionary stance. Although he politely attended church or joined in family prayers when visiting a missionary home, he never converted to Christianity. "The King seems to lack a sense of sin," one missionary complained.

While the king had his doubts about Puritan morality, he was a strong supporter of education from the beginning of his reign. With other ali'i, he required his people to learn to read and write. Literacy was one of the Western tools he willingly chose in a lifetime of choices forced on him by the increasing invasion of foreign powers.

Those powers also forced him to modernize the feudal-style chiefdom his father had left. The kingdom was always at risk as foreign governments annexed small and unprepared nations around the Pacific. In one close call in 1843, British warship captain Lord George Paulet threatened to fire on Honolulu if the king did not pay claims made by British residents. Paulet's escalating demands finally forced Kauikeaouli to cede the kingdom to Great Britain. For the next few months, the king and his advisor, former missionary Dr. Gerrit Judd, quietly resisted Paulet's increasingly harsh rule; at one point, the king went by canoe from Lāhainā to Waikīkī to sign papers in the middle of the night, credentials for a secret emissary to London.

In the meantime, the British government had updated its policy on the Pacific Islands, instructing its far-flung Navy to respect and support the sovereignty of native governments while dealing fairly to protect its own citizens. When the British commander of the Pacific, Admiral Sir Thomas Richards, read the policy, he sailed immediately from the west coast of South America to Hawai'i, reversed the cessation, and sent Paulet on his way.

In a speech celebrating the restoration and Britain's recognition of Hawaiian sovereignty,

Kamehameha III

Kauikeaouli uttered the phrase that has become the motto of Hawai'i: *Ua mau ke ea o ka 'āina i ka pono,* which may be translated "The life [or sovereignty] of the land is perpetuated in righteousness."

Incidents such as this made clear that the kingdom must match its governance to other nations if it were to survive, resulting in a careful study by the chiefs and their *haole* advisors of Western law and the establishment of a constitution and other laws. In the 1840s, often from Lāhainā, Kauikeaouli transformed his kingdom from a feudal chiefdom to a constitutional monarchy, eventually gaining recognition of the kingdom's independence from the great powers.

Not everything went as desired. The *Māhele,* which solved some problems by making private landownership possible, had unintended consequences, leaving many commoners landless and poverty stricken. The king himself often was handicapped by his chronic drinking, whose effects eventually killed him at age forty.

But Kauikeaouli had successfully steered his nation through unknown and troubled waters, always with an eye to the benefit of his subjects. And he had maintained his divine status in his private life, refusing to let outsiders tell him how a king of Hawai'i should live. Kauikeaouli would be remembered by his people as *Ka Mō'ī Lokomaika'i*—the kind, generous, and good-hearted king.

THE WHALING ERA

*We're homeward bound from the Arctic Ground with a good
  ship taut and free
And we won't give a damn when we drink our rum with the
  girls of Old Maui
Rolling down to old Maui, me boys, rolling down to old Maui
We're homeward bound from the Arctic ground, rolling down
  to Old Maui.*
  —Whalers' Song

Lāhainā from the anchorage, circa 1850
Benson John Lossing & William Barritt (engravers)

As early as the 1790s, the favorable conditions in Lāhainā's 'Alalākeiki Channel drew sea captains. Nearby islands shielded ships there from gales, and the sea bottom held an anchor well in this channel, which early maritime visitors called the Lāhainā Roads. Commerce with outsiders began when fur-trading vessels stopped by on trips between Northwest America and Canton, seeking fresh food and water. For a time, beginning in 1810, traders added to their freight the native *'iliahi*— fragrant sandalwood beloved by the Chinese. Kamehameha controlled the trade, but after his death the chiefs overharvested the trees, buying Western goods for themselves while forcing commoners to neglect their *lo'i* to haul *'iliahi* from the forests. Sandalwood was scarce by the late 1820s, and Hawai'i was left with nothing to trade for cash and goods.

Whaling took up the slack, bringing a surge of activity to this quiet village by the sea. New England whalers had devastated whale populations in the Atlantic, so they turned west to hunt the sperm whales of Japan and Alaska. Beginning in 1819, whalers visited Hawai'i each spring and fall to take a break from hunting whales in the North and South Pacific.

Every year, more ships arrived in Lāhainā, drawn by the easy anchorage, the pleasant conditions, and the famous Irish potatoes grown in Kula (a favorite of New England whalermen, who preferred them to the Hawaiians' sweet potato). Their presence twice a year completely transformed the peaceful village, turning it at times into a party, at times a battleground, with as many as fifteen hundred sailors on the streets. "There's no God west of Cape Horn," whalers claimed. After months in cramped quarters, suffering from extreme boredom as they waited for the cry "Thar she blows!" and from hard, dangerous labor as they caught and dismembered their giant prey, Lāhainā was every sailor's dream.

Anyone with something to sell was happy to see the ships arrive, bringing sailors eager to spend cash and their captains ready to trade for fresh water, produce, and meat. Business boomed with the ships' need for sail makers, blacksmiths, and carpenters. Whaleboats cruised the canal (now Canal Street, along one side of Banyan Square) to buy provisions from sellers who set up shop along its length. Captains hired husky Hawaiian men to roll empty barrels up to the Spring House near the mission home, fill them with fresh water, and return them to the ships. The spring's pump sounded all day, a Baldwin daughter recalled.

The American Mission and ship captains pitched in with donations

After months of dangerous labor, whalers looked forward to their time in Lāhainā. Notice the man lying on the whale carcass.
Nantucket Historical Association

to build a two-story building next to the Baldwin's home to house the Masters' Reading Room, a sort of officers' club equipped with books, newspapers, and magazines. Officers could keep an eye on the town and the roadstead through a telescope at their upstairs retreat. Restored and maintained by Lāhainā Restoration Foundation, the building still stands.

Despite the profits, the whaling business had many ill effects on Lāhainā. Forests were stripped for firewood. The kingdom's first mosquitos arrived in a whale ship's water cask. Worst of all was the

Probably built for Kamehameha III, this 1833 building began as a store and inn for visiting sailors—and a retreat for the king far from the missionaries and Christian chiefs at Waineʻe. A decade later, the U.S. government leased it as a hospital for sick and injured sailors, and it's still known as the Seamen's Hospital. This photo was taken before it was restored and leased for private use.
Library of Congress, HABS HI, 5-LAHA, 10-2

effect on the Hawaiian population. Women sold their bodies for cash and goods, and some sailed away with sea captains, willingly or not. Hawaiian men, with voyaging in their genes and a lifetime on the water, joined ship crews, some never to return. Venereal disease contracted by the women and the loss of able-bodied men accelerated the population loss already wreaking havoc among the Hawaiian people.

Alcohol was a big problem. In the early days of whaling, strict rules established by the chiefs and enforced by Governor Hoapili prohibited alcohol ashore, and many captains agreed with this stance. After the death of Hoapili, in 1840, liquor laws were loosened and riotous behavior returned. In 1844, a "respectable resident of Lahaina" reported, hundreds of drunken sailors and natives fought with stones and clubs in close combat. "It is positively unsafe to live in Lāhainā with licensed grog shops," the resident complained. To help control unruly sailors, the Lāhainā Prison, Hale Paʻahao, was built with coral blocks from the old fort next to the harbor.

In 1846, during the heyday of whaling, records show 429 ship arrivals at Lāhainā. Some of these were ships returning twice in one year, so the actual number of individual vessels is uncertain. Still, there were hundreds of them, all filled with sailors ready to spend money on shore leave.

But the boom was not to last. Kerosene distilled from newly drilled North American oil wells replaced whale oil in lamps. Many whaling ships were converted for war use during the U.S. Civil War. In 1871, thirty-three whaling ships were lost in the Arctic, trapped in the ice floes north of Bering Strait. Years of hunting had ravaged the whale population, making the remaining animals harder to find. Ships at anchor dwindled to one or two a year, and the American consul, who had dealt with the troubles of visiting seamen, was called home. The whale ships stopped coming, Lāhainā went back to its life as a sleepy little village, and its residents joined the rest of Hawai'i in searching for a new way to make a living. The industry they founded, sugar growing, would shape Lāhainā and all of Hawai'i for the next century and a half.

Hawaii State Archives

GETTING THERE

The steep *pali* (cliffs) along the southwest coast of West Maui make travel by land a challenge. To avoid the peaks and valleys of the rugged coastline, ancient hikers cut across the tops of the mountains on what is today known as the Old Lāhainā Pali Trail (opposite page). It probably was part of the *Alaloa o Maui,* a round-the-island trail build by King Piʻilani and his son Kihaʻapiʻilani. The trail was rebuilt in the 1800s as a foot and horse trail, and reopened in the 1990s as a hiking trail under the state's *Nā Ala Hele* program.

In the early 1900s, prison laborers built a narrow, one-lane dirt road that could be used by those new-fangled automobiles. By 1925, the road had been expanded to two lanes, but still was a challenging drive, with 115 hairpin turns. The highway, with its spectacular views, earned the nickname Amalfi Drive, after the famous coastal road in Italy.

The Pali Highway offered a wider and less dramatic drive, but kept the spectacular views. Hawai'i's first public tunnel for vehicles, called the "*puka* (hole) through the *pali*," helped open the way in 1951. As you drive the modern highway, keep an eye on the mountainside for remnants of the original "Amalfi Drive" highway, including a segment above the tunnel opening.

Lāhainā's great banyan tree was planted behind the courthouse on April 24, 1873, by Sheriff William Owen Smith to commemorate the fiftieth anniversary of the founding of Lāhainā's Christian mission. The eight-foot stripling Sheriff Smith planted has become a quarter-acre-sized landmark where residents and visitors gather in the shade of its amazing branches.

A member of the fig family, originally from India, the banyan's branches drop aerial roots that eventually touch the ground and grow into new tree trunks. Over many years, Lāhainā gardeners shaped the growth of the tree by trimming some of the roots and encouraging others to grow, hanging large glass jars filled with water to pull the roots straight toward the earth.

The largest banyan in the United States, the tree stands more than sixty feet high, with sixteen major trunks, as well as the original. The Maui County Arborist Committee maintains the tree's health and shape, and Lāhainā Restoration Foundation takes care of the grounds, now known as Banyan Tree Park.
Hawai'i State Archives

SUGAR BRINGS WORKERS FROM AFAR

The multicultural Hawai'i we know today got an early start when American and European sailors arrived in Hawai'i and decided to stay. Their marriages to Hawaiian women produced hapa-haole (half-foreign) families, many of whose descendants still carry the names of those early Caucasian immigrants. While these newcomers came one at a time, great waves of immigrants began to arrive in the mid-1800s to fill the need for workers in the sugarcane fields.

Chinese lads rest from their travels. Lāhainā Restoration Foundation

Before Western contact, Hawaiians raised sugar as part of a mixed-crop system and chewed the sweet cane stalks. New arrivals began processing cane into molasses and syrup, and occasionally sugar, in the early 1800s. Lāhaināluna Seminary graduate David Malo made molasses and syrup in Lāhainā in the 1840s.

As the whaling industry vanished, farmers and businessmen searching for profitable crops discovered that processed sugar could survive the long voyage to American markets. The *Māhele ‘Āina* had allowed them to amass fee-simple lands; here at last was a promising cash crop to make that land pay.

Commercial sugar growing in Lāhainā began about 1860, with the establishment of the Lāhainā Sugar Company, which encouraged sugar cultivation on plots formerly devoted to growing vegetables for whaling-ship crews. In 1863, a former whaler named James Campbell and his partner, Henry Turton, founded the Pioneer Mill Company. They took over the assets of the Lāhainā Sugar Company and later of the West Maui Sugar Association, established by Kamehameha V and partners to assist natives in growing sugar. Pioneer Mill Company, one of many sugar plantations that would control Hawai‘i economic, political, and social life for decades, came to dominate the West Maui landscape. By 1935, the company cultivated more than ten thousand acres of sugar on lands surrounding Lāhainā town.

Cane fields covered thousands of acres of West Maui landscape.
Naoki Kutsunai, Lāhainā Restoration Foundation

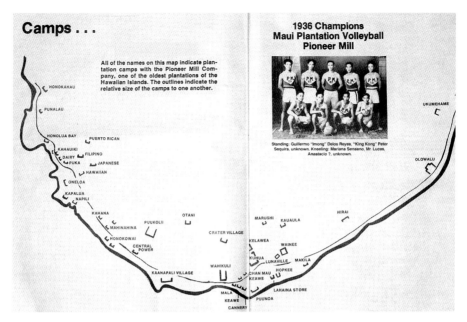

Sports competitions of all kinds were a big deal in Pioneer Mill plantation camps scattered along the West Maui coast. Winners within camp leagues would go on to play the champs from other plantations, and in 1936, the Pioneer Mill volleyball team took top place. The Maui News

When sugar became a major crop, the Hawaiian population had been shrinking for decades as one epidemic after another swept across the Islands. For the plantations, these losses meant there simply were not enough Hawaiians to work the growing sugar plantations. Many who survived preferred their traditional life of fishing and kalo cultivation to dusty plantation work in the midday sun. So plantations began to import laborers, creating a unique multiethnic population. Starting with Chinese from Canton in 1852, thousands came to work in Hawai'i fields.

By 1924, Pioneer Mill Company maintained forty-two "camps," or plantation villages, as homes for workers from China, Japan, the Portuguese Azores and Madeira Islands, Korea, Puerto Rico, and the Philippines, along with some Native Hawaiians and immigrants from the United States and various European countries. Each group that came brought its own food, language, and customs. In the camps, individual ethnic groups lived separately from others. It was easier for newcomers to live close to neighbors who shared their background and language, but it also allowed the plantation bosses to set groups against each other at times of labor unrest.

Front Street in the early 1900s Lāhainā Restoration Foundation

A PLANTATION COMMUNITY

Lāhainā was the business and commercial center for all of West Maui, the main town of a region connected to the rest of the island by a narrow, winding road perched on the Pali to the south. In the early twentieth century, mom-and-pop stores lined Front Street, selling everything from saimin to fresh fish. Entrepreneurial immigrant families (mostly Japanese) whose plantation contracts had ended opened little businesses—barbershops, bakeries, fish markets, and small restaurants. Front Street's stores were as important to community life as they were to the economy, a place to meet friends and "talk story."

It was a typical small town, with churches and dances, parades, Boy Scouts, and football games. Unlike most American small towns, however, Lāhainā was a place where kids learned to swim off the beach in front of the courthouse or caught fish from the back porch of an oceanfront store. The old seaport maintained its connection to the ocean, the highway to the rest of the territory, so generous with fish but occasionally, as in the dreadful 1946 tsunami, threatening and destructive.

Above the town, and for miles on either end of it, Pioneer Mill Company's fields were rocky but favorable to the growth of sugarcane.

Some of the best fields kept producing cane without replowing or replanting for as long as ten years. In 1910, Pioneer Mill Company employed sixteen hundred, half of them contract laborers and half of them day workers. Their children attended schools on the plantation and in Lāhainā, and by 1914, the company sponsored a kindergarten for nearly a thousand young children.

In a process that became more mechanized as the years went by, workers began a new sugar crop by planting short pieces of cane stalk. The plantation developed an extensive ditch collection system and wells to bring water from mountain streams to irrigate this thirsty crop, which requires one million gallons to produce a ton of sugar. The first well on Maui was drilled for Pioneer Mill Company in 1883.

Hop Wo Store was known for its Chinese specialties and fresh bread baked in an oven fueled by kiawe *wood. It remained in business through the 1960s. The carriage is parked outside Kato Fish Market next door.*
M. Kadotani, Lāhainā Restoration Foundation

At harvest time, after two years of growth, cane fields were burned to remove the leaves, leaving the juice-filled stems behind. Machete-wielding workers (and later harvesting machines) cut the cane and loaded it onto trains or trucks that carried the harvested cane to the mill. The cane's root system remained underground and sprouted anew to produce another crop.

Plantation trains delivered harvested cane to the mill, where it was first washed to remove dirt and rocks, then fed between giant rollers

Trains hauled cane across the plantation to the mill. Lāhainā Restoration Foundation

turned by enormous gear wheels. The rollers squeezed sugar juice from the cane. Leftover cane fiber, known as bagasse, became fuel for the plantation's steam-generating plant. The juice was clarified by the addition of slaked lime, then condensed by boiling to a thick syrup, and finally separated by centrifugal force into raw sugar and molasses. Raw sugar was shipped to the mainland to be refined into white sugar, and molasses often became livestock feed.

Pioneer Mill was almost a self-contained community, needing workers for everything from bookkeeping to medical care to delivering milk from the plantation's dairy, as well as jobs more directly related to running a sugar plantation—carpenters, mechanics, blacksmiths to shoe horses and mules, engineers and brakemen to run the plantation railroad, irrigation teams to build and install irrigation systems and manage the flow of water into the fields that stretched ten miles along the coast. Women, too, worked for the plantation, usually doing less strenuous jobs like weeding, hoeing, and cutting cane into pieces to be replanted.

Pioneer Mill Company dominated Lāhainā and much of West Maui for more than a century. Lāhainā Restoration Foundation

The original Pioneer Mill Hospital, shown here about 1908. The plantation provided health care and other basic services to its employees.
Lāhainā Restoration Foundation

Youngsters took on summer jobs in the fields to supplement family income, and during World War II Lāhaināluna High School students spent one day a week in the fields instead of at school, making up for lost labor as men went to war. None of the jobs paid well in the prewar years, but the plantation's paternalistic provision of "perquisites" like housing made things livable, if not luxurious, old-timers remember.

Workers line up on payday, each with his bango, *a metal tag with a number used for everything from recording an employee's work history to charging goods at the company store.* Lāhainā Restoration Foundation

Horses and mules played a part in sugar farming. Hawai'i State Archives

Plantation employees lived close to their work sites in the villages known as camps, scattered from Ukumehame to Honokōhau. Life was simple and rural, with flourishing gardens, chicken coops, and outhouses sometimes set over a stream of water that carried waste to a cesspool. A central bathhouse might serve an entire camp, often with a Japanese-style hot tub known as a *furo*.

Families paid a small amount of rent but received free electricity, kerosene, water, and also medical care from the plantation. They cooled food with ice delivered by the Lāhainā Ice Company, headquartered on the shore near the harbor. Most families grew their own vegetables and raised chickens, rabbits, or even pigs, which were good for a little extra income, as well as meat. Families didn't need much in the way of groceries, but what they did came from the plantation's Lāhainā Store on Front Street, which sent salesmen to take orders and then delivered food, which might include a hundred-pound bag of rice for five dollars.

Though life was difficult in many ways, plantation camp families lived in peaceful, cooperative communities. When their garden or fishnet produced a surplus, they shared it with neighbors, and the neighbors did the same. Kids roamed freely, usually barefoot, heading up the mountain to swim in the irrigation ditches or down to the ocean to spearfish. Sports were a big part of local life, with competition between camp teams and in the Plantation League against teams from around the island. Holidays featured plenty to eat, each home welcoming guests to sample their specialty. The plantation provided trucks to take everyone to Central Maui for the island's big annual event, the Maui County Fair.

Plantation supervisors, known as *luna,* lived more upscale lives than the workers. One such family, the part-Hawaiian Fardens, had a long-lasting influence on the community and the culture. Pā'ia-born Charles Kekua Farden attended Punahou School in Honolulu, then returned to his hometown to work on the plantation. He met Annie Kahalepouli Bastel Shaw, known as the "Songbird of Mauna Olu" (a girls' school near Pā'ia), and the pair married after Annie's graduation in 1897. Two years, later they moved to Annie's hometown, Lāhainā, where Charles began work at Pioneer Mill.

Riders enjoy the "Lāhainā Road" (now Front Street) near the shore in 1905.
Photo courtesy Rob Ratkowski

The family built a 5,000-square-foot, six-bedroom house at Puamana, on the shoreline just south of Mokuhinia. Here, they reared a dozen children, each of whom planted a coconut tree along the shoreline and tended it carefully.

Puamana was at the edge of the old *ali'i* center of Lāhainā. In the early twentieth century, this neighborhood retained its character as a home for the elite, populated by plantation executives and professionals instead of the chiefs of old. The Farden family home became a focus of manager-level social life, with parties, luncheons, and holiday celebrations, as well as *pau hana* (after work) gatherings of Mr. Farden and his plantation supervisor colleagues.

Charles, who had been at Punahou during the overthrow of the Hawaiian monarchy, determined to face the future by raising his children as Americans, and chose not to teach them the Hawaiian language or customs, though the family continued to sing Hawaiian songs.

All the Farden children were musical, but it was Emma who braved her father's displeasure to learn the hula. She found teachers who trained her in the ancient dance and its traditions. Seeing his daughter's talent, Charles was persuaded to relent. She continued to study hula and taught her brothers and sisters to dance.

As an adult, after teaching all day at Kamehameha III Elementary School, Emma Farden Sharpe would teach and perform hula. A lively redhead, she became famous on Maui, particularly for her entertainment of troops during World War II. Her *halau* (hula school), called Puamana, performed for many years at the new hotels built in Kā'anapali starting in the early 1960s.

Meanwhile, the other siblings also were singing and performing, and sister Irmgard began composing songs that included the well-known song in praise of the family home, *Puamana*. She recruited her father to help with the Hawaiian words, and Emma created a hula to go with them.

After the elder Fardens' deaths in the 1940s, the family sold their

Emma Farden Sharpe, seated at right, led her family in reclaiming the musical and performing heritage of her Hawaiian ancestors. She is shown here at the 1957 dedication of Hale Hō'ike'eke, a museum in the former home of Wailuku missionaries Edward and Caroline Bailey. Maui Historical Society

old home to Pioneer Mill. In the mid-1960s, the site of the Pioneer Mill manager's house, at the far end of the Front Street neighborhood, was developed as a condominium project. The developer asked the Farden children's permission to use the name "Puamana," and the siblings agreed. Today, many people mistakenly think of the condominium as the site of the Farden home, but the original site is on the Lahaina end of the residential stretch of Front Street.

The Farden family influence continues, with the annual Emma Farden Sharpe Hula Festival in Lāhainā and continued musical performances by the grandchildren of Charles and Annie. What do these singers call their group? Why, "Puamana," of course.

Mokuhinia and other wetland areas around Lāhainā were nearly dried up by the time this picture was taken, in 1905. Photo courtesy Rob Ratkowski

CANE TAKES THE WATER

Sugar cultivation forever changed the traditional verdant Lāhainā landscape. The streams and springs that previously had watered the town dried up as the plantation built an irrigation ditch system in the mountains above, diverting natural water flow to their fields. Without fresh water, kalo farming became impossible. Waterways once traversed by canoe disappeared. The spring-fed pond that for centuries had been the center of Lāhainā ali'i life became an unpleasant-smelling, mosquito-infested swamp. In 1914, with the pragmatism of the times, civic and business leaders had the sedge-choked pond filled with soil and coral rubble for "hygienic" reasons. The newly filled pond became Malu-'ulu-o-Lele County Park in 1918. Generations would use this park to play softball and tennis, on ground that once was sacred to the chiefs and their ancestral goddess Kihawahine.

Sailors filled Front Street when the U.S. Pacific Fleet was in town.
Naoki Kutsunai, Lāhainā Restoration Foundation

WAR CHANGES EVERYTHING

The quiet plantation town grew busy again when World War II transformed Maui into an armed training camp, with thousands of military personnel stationed around the island and rolls of barbed wire protecting beaches from invasion. The military had been visiting for several years before World War II began. Lāhainā Roads was an alternative anchorage for Pearl Harbor. Each year, a U.S. fleet of aircraft carriers, destroyers, battleships, submarines, and other vessels called at Lāhainā for war maneuvers. Sailors on leave put ashore in small boats to be met by Mauians who welcomed them with snacks and entertained them with hula. Though most of the training facilities were located on other parts of the island, Lāhainā saw its share of off-duty service members, businesses bustled again, and Lāhainā residents pitched in like everyone else in Hawai'i to help in the war effort.

The United States Pacific Fleet began visiting Lāhainā in the early 1930s for annual war maneuvers. This photo of the fleet at anchor includes some Lāhainā landmarks. Bottom left is the playing field of Malu-'ulu-o-Lele County Park, formerly the royal pond, Mokuhinia. Lower center right is Pioneer Mill. The light-colored rectangle near the shore at right is Baldwin Packers, where pineapple grown in Honolua was canned. Nearby Mala Wharf eventually was abandoned because of continuous strong cross currents and storm damage.
Lāhainā Restoration Foundation

After the war, though agriculture still dominated the Lāhainā economy, the town began a slow decline. Even before the war, laborers had begun to demand better working conditions. When peace returned, a series of strikes led to a restructuring of the plantations. These began with a territory-wide strike in 1946 that broke the back of the "perquisite" system. In Lāhainā, the strike lasted 123 days, and Kula farmers donated vegetables to the soup kitchens that fed striking workers and their families.

The strike resulted in higher wages, an end to racial discrimination and segregation, and new benefits such as vacations and sick leave. The plantations were ready to get out of the business of providing housing to their workers, so they gave employees first priority to purchase newly built houses in the community. The plantation camps began to close.

Life for the average plantation worker gradually became easier, and younger generations, educated in public schools and universities, moved beyond the cane fields. Still, Lāhainā continued in its placid, small-town mode, centered on the plantation that kept its people employed and the fields green above the town.

Lāhainā residents march in a Memorial Day parade about 1943 to honor Lāhainā men lost in the war. Japanese-Americans were particularly eager to prove their patriotism after the December 7, 1941, bombing of Pearl Harbor, and young men enlisted in droves. At home, everyone worked hard to make up for their lost labor and to help with defense efforts. Even youngsters dug air-raid trenches, collected scrap metal, grew vegetables, and volunteered to weed the sugarcane fields. Lāhainā Restoration Foundation

WELCOMING THE WORLD

Things would change along this whole coastline beginning in the early 1960s. All of Hawai'i was seeing an increase in tourism after statehood and the beginning of commercial jet travel. More visitors meant more hotels, and then condominiums as some people returned wanting a more homelike experience, and, finally, dwellings for those who had decided to make Maui their permanent residence.

Fortunately, as development began in Kā'anapali, preservation efforts protected Lāhainā's historic character and many existing historic sites in town. In 1962, the Lāhainā Restoration Foundation formed, with the goal of restoring and maintaining the historical and cultural assets of the community. The next year, Lāhainā was named a National Historic Landmark, and in 1967, the County of Maui established two Historic Districts to preserve the prevailing historical atmosphere and architecture

Pioneer Hotel, founded in 1901, with the Lāhainā Courthouse at right. The hotel was renamed the Pioneer Inn in the 1950s. For many years it was the only hotel on the West side. Library of Congress, HABS HI, 5-LAHA, 7--10

along much of Front Street and in the residential neighborhoods behind it.

The Lāhainā Restoration Foundation's first major project was the old missionary Baldwin Home, which opened to visitors in 1965. The foundation continues to manage Lāhainā's most important historical buildings and areas, from the Seamen's Hospital on the north end of Front Street to extensive written and photographic archives at Hale Pa'i, to the Banyan Tree and the Old Lāhainā Courthouse, with a museum upstairs commemorating the history of the town.

Lāhainā's quaint streets filled with visitors as the new industry of tourism grew. Everywhere in Hawai'i, energy was shifting away from agriculture. Lāhainā had been a plantation town for more than a century, the rhythms of its days and its seasons dictated by the needs of the sugar crop. But in 1999, Pioneer Mill Company harvested its last crop as the Hawai'i sugar industry faltered, unable to match cheap worldwide sugar prices.

Jim Luckey demonstrates a replica of the original printing press, made for Hale Pa'i, the old printing house on the Lāhaināluna High School campus. Luckey was executive director of the Lāhainā Restoration Foundation for twenty-five years beginning in 1972, leading efforts to restore many of the town's historic buildings. He pioneered the concept of "adaptive use," in which a restored building is put to use for contemporary needs.
Lāhainā Restoration Foundation

The Pioneer Mill smokestack was a Lāhainā landmark, long used by mariners as a navigational guide. Each Christmas, two illuminated stars atop the smokestack marked the season. After Pioneer Mill closed, the mill buildings were demolished, but the community worked with Lāhainā Restoration Foundation to restore this lofty monument to the importance of sugar in Lāhainā history, repairing and reinforcing its walls and replacing a "crown" previously removed for safety reasons.

The Old Lāhainā Courthouse, built in 1860, was home to the post office and other official services when this picture was taken. Now managed by the Lāhainā Restoration Foundation, its second floor houses the Lāhainā Heritage Museum, with displays that trace the history of the town through the centuries.
Library of Congress, HABS HI,5-LAHA,6—1

TOURISM TAKES OVER

The community leaders of the 1950s who helped establish the Maui tourism industry probably had no idea how successful their efforts would be, nor how much they would change the island lifestyle. In those days, Pioneer Mill's sugar plantation still dominated Lāhainā, and to the north, pineapple thrived, first planted in 1912 on the Baldwin family's Honolua Ranch.

In the decade after World War II, Maui's plantation-based economy had struggled to meet rising labor costs and increasing foreign competition. Young people were leaving the island in search of opportunity; between 1950 and 1960, population dropped from 40,103 to 35,717.

So in the mid-1900s, business and community leaders began to recreate Lāhainā as a tourist destination. The twin explosions set off by their vision, of visitors and of population growth, began with the development of Kā'anapali as a world-class resort.

Puʻu Kekaʻa (Black Rock) is shown here as it existed in 1958 and on the opposite page as it looked after the Sheraton Maui was built a few years later. The buildings visible through the trees in the older picture were part of the set for a movie filmed there, Twilight of the Gods.
Alexander & Baldwin Sugar Museum

In the early part of the twentieth century, though the land along the shore wasn't suitable for cane cultivation, Kāʻanapali played a part in exporting sugar. Remnants of an old pier remain on the north side of Puʻu Kekaʻa (Black Rock). Railroad tracks ran between the cane fields and the pier, where the plantation loaded processed sugar onto tugboats, which towed barges out to ships headed to the mainland. The barges also delivered supplies for the plantation camps. One of those camps was on what are now the Royal Lāhainā Resort grounds. The workers who lived there oversaw the loading of sugar onto barges.

Sugar-loading operations transferred to Lāhainā in the 1930s, the workers moved away, and the land, with its protein-rich *kiawe* trees, was left to grazing cattle and the occasional local pleasure seeker. For the next two decades, Kāʻanapali was a place where families picnicked or fished. A road led halfway up Puʻu Kekaʻa to a fuel-oil tank, and

The Sheraton Maui was built on the famous Puʻu Kekaʻa, also known as Black Rock. Courtesy Sheraton Maui Resort & Spa

Lāhainā in the 1970s was still a place where rents were low and shoreline residents could fish off the back porch. Tom Russo photo, Barbara Long collection

from there an explorer could fight to the top through weeds and brush to enjoy the eternal blue view. So it remained until the mid-1950s, when American Factors, the parent company of the Pioneer Mill sugar plantation, commissioned a study that forecast the potential success of a resort. Kā'anapali was off and running.

The new project created terrific excitement on the island. It isn't often that you see an exclamation point in a newspaper headline, but the editor couldn't restrain himself. "Kaanapali Resort Area To Cost $36 Million! Lahaina Beach Project Takes In 395 Acres!" proclaimed *The Maui News* front page of April 14, 1957. The promise of a new commercial enterprise on an island in the economic doldrums was a big story indeed.

Mauians had been talking about the potential of tourism for years, seeing verdant 'Īao Valley and the dramatic peak of Haleakalā as visitor magnets. Talk turned to reality when "Amfac" realized that it owned a vacationer's dream destination: nearly three miles of pristine white sand bordering a turquoise ocean, with views of the islands of Lāna'i and Moloka'i floating on the horizon and lush fields of sugarcane stretching up the slopes of the scenic West Maui Mountains.

The streets were quiet and the buildings needed paint on Front Street in 1973.
Tom Russo photo, Barbara Long collection

Despite the region's natural beauty, it required foresight to imagine a flourishing Maui tourist industry before 1959, when statehood and the introduction of jet flights from the U.S. Mainland began to draw large quantities of visitors to Hawai'i. Lāhainā in the 1950s was a sleepy plantation town where unfamiliar faces were rare and the Pioneer Hotel (built in 1901) provided minimal accommodations. Tourism belonged in Waikīkī; the "Neighbor Islands" were a backwater, and few people outside of Hawai'i had even heard of Maui.

But executives of American Factors recognized Kā'anapali's potential and were willing to risk investing in a long-term plan for development. They hauled in tons of dirt from Olowalu to build a golf course on the dry rocky land behind the beach. Amfac built the resort's first two hotels—the Royal Lāhainā Beach Club and the Sheraton Maui— and initially leased the land on which other accommodations were built. By the time hotel and condominium operators were allowed to purchase their sites, Amfac's high standards for design and open space were well established. Kā'anapali became the world's first master-planned resort community.

The Royal Lāhainā opened in December 1962, the Sheraton Maui a

On a rare rainy day, the Lāhainā Whaling Spree Parade moves down Front Street. The Whaling Spree started in 1962 as a family-friendly event with costumes and beard-growing contests, canoe races and dancing. Unfortunately, it lived up to its name and had to be shut down in 1971, after suffering for years from progressively worse alcohol-fueled misbehavior.
Maui Historical Society

month later. The Sheraton was an "upside-down" hotel, with its lobby at the top of the famous Puʻu Kekaʻa and rooms in a series of hanging gardens on the sheer face of the rock. A third venue, Kāʻanapali Hotel (now Kāʻanapali Beach Hotel) was built in seven months to open in time for the Canada Cup international golf championship on the Royal Kāʻanapali Golf Course, which had been designed by Robert Trent Jones Sr. That event, in December 1964, drew VIPs like Bing Crosby, Laurance Rockefeller, and the Duke of Windsor to watch American champions Jack Nicklaus and Arnold Palmer play golfers from around the world.

On the north end of the resort, a private landing strip opened in 1962, next to what became known as "Airport Beach." The bar at the top of the airport's little terminal, the Windsock Lounge, was a favorite hangout. The airstrip closed in 1987.

By the end of the twentieth century, tourism was the economic engine of Hawai'i, and visitor-oriented businesses dominated Front Street. This contemporary photo shows one of the busiest corners in town.
Sjoerd Witteveen photo

As landscaping and construction were transforming Kāʻanapali, the old town of Lāhainā received a careful facelift. Lāhainā would become a favorite spot for Kāʻanapali guests looking for nearby local flavor and a glimpse of the past.

Kāʻanapali more than lived up to the vision of its founders. The resort that pioneered tourism on Maui is world famous, attracting more than half a million visitors each year to 4,800 hotel rooms, condominium suites, and villas. And as a destination for shopping, dining, whale watching, and scores of other activities, Lāhainā welcomes thousands of visitors to its historic streets.

The strategy of early planners was to create beautiful resorts (Kāʻanapali was followed by Wailea and Kapalua) where tourists would spend their time. But the visitors could not be contined; they soon discovered the rest of an island filled with a variety of microclimates, activities, and scenery. Tourism overtook agriculture as the top industry. By 2015, tourists numbered more than two and a half million a year, and Maui County population had more than quadrupled from its 1960 total to some 165,000.

Alongside the thousands of visitors to Lāhainā are longtime residents, including some whose ancestors lived here in the days when the great *moʻo* Kihawahine inhabited the grotto under Mokuhinia Pond and some whose ancestors arrived to farm the sugar fields that eventually destroyed the waterways filling that pond. Behind the busy tourist streets, the daily life of the town goes on in quiet neighborhoods, schools, and businesses, among families and organizations for whom this will always be home.

At one time, it seemed the ancient and sacred history of this place had been forgotten. But today, ever-changing, persisting through centuries, Lāhainā has remembered its past. Early restoration efforts often focused on the whaling and missionary days of the nineteenth century—the sometimes raucous Whaling Spree of the 1960s is one example. But today, Lāhainā residents are keenly aware of the importance of their town in the centuries before and the decades after the Hawaiʻi Island

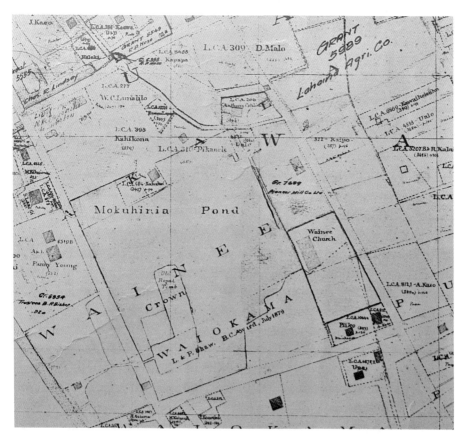

This old map shows the island Mokuʻula, marked with the word "crown," within the square shape of Mokuhinia Pond.

A plaque explains the history of Mokuʻula and Mokuhinia, while a standing stone provides a focal point for contemporary ceremonies.

warriors of Kamehameha I conquered the rest of the Island chain.

Memories of Mokuʻula began to resurface in the late 1980s, after the Kāʻanapali Beach Hotel launched its Poʻokela Program to educate employees about Hawaiian culture and history. In the early 1990s, an archaeological investigation of the pond Mokuhinia and the island Mokuʻula by the anthropology department of the Bernice Pauahi Bishop Museum confirmed the existence of the island beneath the coral-and-soil fill of the county recreational park. That first dig found remnants of a stone retaining wall at the island's edge and of a wooden pier. Mokuʻula was placed on both the state and national Registers of Historic Places.

Following the first archaeological dig and the publication of Dr. Paul Christiaan Klieger's book *Mokuʻula: Maui's Sacred Island,* interest in the mysterious ancient site grew. In 1998, leaders of Rapa Nui (Easter Island) in the southeast Pacific visited to participate in a ceremony that included representatives of other Polynesian societies, as well as Maui's Hawaiian community. The Rapa Nui group recognized Mokuʻula as an

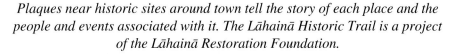

Plaques near historic sites around town tell the story of each place and the people and events associated with it. The Lāhainā Historic Trail is a project of the Lāhainā Restoration Foundation.

ancestral home, known in their traditions as Moto Ura.

The findings under the Malu-ʻulu-o-Lele Park spurred formation of a group dedicated to reviving the wetland and restoring the ancient structures whose foundations lay buried under the park. Friends of Mokuʻula was formed in 1995. Eventually, the Friends group was granted a lease and license to occupy parts of the county park property. The ball field was closed, though tennis courts and restrooms remained in use. A platform was built on one edge of the old ball field, with stone retaining walls around an earthen terrace topped with a standing stone, a gathering place for ceremonial events.

Since that time, the Friends of Mokuʻula have worked to better understand the treasure buried beneath former parkland, hosting several archaeological studies that used modern technology and techniques to peer beneath the surface. Their goal is to restore the Islands' premier cultural site to its former glory, a reminder to all of the long history of this resilient and enduring town.

ACKNOWLEDGEMENTS

This book owes much to many people, beginning with its very title. Inez MacPhee Ashdown published a booklet called *The Story of Lahaina* in 1947. Several years ago, I was asked to consider updating the original book, but both knowledge and attitudes have changed in the decades since Inez wrote, so I decided to start from scratch. I trust that Inez would not mind my borrowing her title. It was Inez who gave me some of my earliest appreciation and understanding of Maui's past as I helped her put together her memoirs when she was in her 80s. Her stories are always in the back of my mind when I observe and write about Maui today. Though not a trained historian, Inez loved and respected the Hawaiian culture at a time when that was not fashionable, and as a result her Hawaiian friends gave her the name 'Āina Kaulana, meaning that she "brought pride to the land."

Several scholars have published writings that contributed greatly to this book. Kepa and Onaona Maly, working as Kumu Pono Associates, produced an in-depth study called *He Wahi Moʻolelo No Kauʻaula A Me Kekāhi 'Āina O Lahaina I Maui (A Collection of Traditions and Historical Accounts of Kauaʻula and Other Lands of Lahaina, Maui)*. Dr. Paul Christiaan Klieger led the original excavation of Mokuʻula and documented that and the history of the area in his book *Mokuʻula: Maui's Sacred Island*. He also authored the first biography of Kamehameha III. Patrick V. Kirsch has written many books about the archaeology and history of Hawaiʻi; I am particularly grateful for *How Chiefs Became Kings,* a study of the founding of a "state" in the Hawaiian Islands. *The Lahainaluna 150th Anniversary Commemorative Book* gave me information on the founding of that historic school.

Photos came from several sources, including Rob Ratkowski, who saved a 1905 photo album from the trash bin and generously shares these wonderful old photos.

Friends also helped, especially Katherine Kamaʻemaʻe Smith, who described for me Lāhainā as it must have appeared to the first settlers. With a deep understanding of West Maui history, Katherine also read and gave me feedback on the first complete draft of the manuscript. Barbara Long, ardent preservationist and former Lāhainā resident, added her suggestions and perspective and lent photos. Karee Carlucci, go-to person for Lāhainā historical tales, was kind enough to read and critique my manuscript. Janie Taylor expertly edited, Bobbie Best proofread, and Cynthia Conrad tweaked pictures and designed pages to make the book beautiful. Haynes Publishing Group graciously granted permission to reprint the history of Kāʻanapali, originally written for their *Kāʻanapali Magazine*.

Perhaps most importantly, Theo Morrison, executive director of the Lāhainā Restoration Foundation, hired me several times over the years to help with historical writing for foundation projects, including for the Old Lāhainā Courthouse Museum, which traces Lāhainā history from its Polynesian beginnings. It was Theo who pointed out the need for a book like this, describing the fantastic history of this little town for the millions who visit as well as those who live here.

Jill Engledow
September 2016

INDEX

ahupua'a (land division), 3
'Alalākeiki Channel, 42
Alaloa o Maui, 46, 46*f*
Alexander, Samuel T., 25
Alexander & Baldwin, 25
ali'i (chiefs), 5–7, 5*f*, 8–16
Amalfi Drive, 46–47, 46*f*, 47*f*
American Board of Commissioners for Foreign Missions, 22, 25, 29
American Factors (Amfac), 68–69
Andrews, Lorrin, 29–30
'aumakua (family god), 10
'auwai (irrigation channels), 2

Baldwin, Charlotte Fowler, 23–24, 23*f*, 26
Baldwin, Dwight, 23–25, 23*f*, 28, 31–32
Baldwin, Henry P., 25, 28
Baldwin Home Museum, 3*f*, 24, 24*f*, 64
Banyan Tree Park, 48, 48*f*, 64
Bird, Isabella, 14
Black Rock (Pu'u Keka'a), 8, 66–67, 66*f*, 67*f*, 69
Breadfruit *('ulu)*, 3–4, 3*f*, 8

Campbell, James, 50
chiefs. See *ali'i*
Christianity, 17–21, 22–33, 31
Cleveland, Richard, 13
coconut, 3, 7, 57
Constitution of 1840, 36
Cook, James, 1*f*, 15, 27

diseases, plagues, and epidemics, 12, 24–25, 27, 44, 51
diversity, ethnic and religious, 33, 49, 49*f*, 51–52

Ebenezera Church, 28. See also Waine'e Church
Edict of Toleration, 33
Emma Farden Sharpe Hula Festival, 59

family god *('aumakua)*, 10
Farden family, 57-59
fish ponds *(loko i'a)*, 10–11
Friends of Moku'ula, 74
Front Street, 14, 24, 33, 52, 52*f*, 56, 57*f*, 59 60, 60*f*, 64, 68*f*, 69*f*, 70*f*

grass houses, 8*f*, 18*f*, 20, 26, 33

Hale Aloha, 25
Hale Hō'ike'eke, 58*f*
Hale Pa'ahao (Lāhainā Prison), 34, 44–45
Hale Pa'i, 30, 30*f*, 64, 64*f*
Hale Piula, 20, 33

Hawaiian Magna Carta, 35–36
heiau (place of worship), 6, 9, 13, 16*f*, 17
Hoapili, 18, 21, 26, 28–29, 44
horses, 13–14, 13*f*
houses, grass, 8*f*, 18*f*, 20, 26, 33

'Īao Valley, 12, 68
'iliahi (sandalwood), 16, 42

Judd, Gerrit, 39

Ka'ahumanu *(kuhina nui)*, 13, 16–17, 19–20, 19*f*, 34–36
Kā'anapali, 65–72
Kā'anapali Beach Hotel, 14, 69–70, 72
Kahekili, 11–12, 15
kahuna (priestly class), 7
Kaka'alaneo, 8
Ka Lama, The Torch, 30
Kalaniopu'u, 15
kalo (taro), 3–4, 4*f*, 6, 11, 13, 16*f*, 18, 23, 37*f*, 51, 59
Kamehameha I (the Great), 11–17, 11*f*, 15*f*, 21–22, 24, 34, 38, 72
Kamehameha II (Liholiho), 10, 13, 16–19, 17*f*, 19*f*
Kamehameha III (Kauikeaouli), 10, 18–22, 19*f*, 27, 33, 35, 38–40, 38*f*, 39*f*, 75
Kamehameha III Elementary School, 18, 58
Kamehameha V, 50
kapa (bark-cloth fabric), 8, 8*f*, 16*f*
kapu system (taboos), 5, 7, 10, 15, 17, 31, 34
Kaua'ula wind, 28
Kauikeaouli (Kamehameha III), 10, 18–22, 19*f*, 27, 33, 35, 38–40, 38*f*, 39*f*, 75
Kaululā'au, 8–9
Kekāuluohi, 10
Keōpūolani, 12–15, 17–23
Keōua, 15
Kepaniwai, 12
Kiha-a-Pi'ilani, 9
Kihawahine, 10, 14, 20, 60, 71
Kīwala'ō, 15
Klieger, Paul Christiaan, 73
kuhina nui. See Ka'ahumanu
kuleana (personal responsibility), 3
kuleana (plot of land), 37–38
Kuleana Act of 1849, 37

Lāhainā
    as capital of Hawaiian kingdom, 17–21
    early history and descriptions of, 1–6, 10–11
    land divisions of, 2*f*
    map of, 16*f*
    meaning of name, 2–3

in modern times, 63–74
 as National Historic Landmark, 63
 as plantation community, 52–59
 restoration of historic sites, 71–74
Lāhainā Courthouse. *See* Old Lāhainā
 Courthouse
Lāhainā Heritage Museum, 65*f*
Lāhaināluna Seminary, 23, 29, 29–31, 29*f*, 35, 50
Lāhainā Moku, 3, 5, 8, 11
Lāhainā Prison (Hale Pa'ahao), 34, 44–45
Lāhainā Restoration Foundation, 43, 48, 63–64
Lāhainā Roads, 21, 42, 60
Lāhainā Store, 56
Lāhainā Sugar Company, 50
land use and ownership, 35, 37–38
laws and lawmaking, 34–40
Liholiho (Kamehameha II), 10, 13, 16–19, 17*f*, 19*f*
literacy (*palapala*), 22, 26–27, 35, 39
lizard goddess. See *mo'o*
lo'i kalo (taro ponds), 4*f*, 11, 16*f*, 37*f*
loko i'a (fish ponds), 10–11
Lua'ehu, 13
Lua'ehu Constitution, 36
Luckey, Jim, 64If
luna (plantation supervisors), 57

Māhele 'Āina, 37–38, 37*f*, 40, 50
maka'āinana (common people), 7, 37–38
Mala Wharf, 61*f*
Malo, David, 29, 31–32, 31*f*, 50
Malu-'ulu-o-Lele County Park, 60, 61*f*, 74
mana (divine power), 7, 13–14, 20–21
Maria Lanakila church, 33
Masters' Reading Room, 43
Menzies, Archibald, 10–11
missionaries, 17–21, 22–33, 32–33. See also *specific names of missionaries*
Mokuhinia Pond, 9–10, 9*f*, 36, 57, 59*f*, 61*f*, 71–73, 72*f*, 73*f*
Moku'ula, 6, 9–10, 20, 72–74, 72*f*, 73*f*
Moku'ula: Maui's Sacred Island (Klieger), 73
mo'o (lizard goddess), 10, 14, 71
mosquitos, 43

Nāhi'ena'ena, 15, 18–20, 19*f*, 38

Old Lāhainā Courthouse, 18, 63*f*, 64, 65*f*
Old Lāhainā Trail, 46, 46*f*
oral traditions, 5–6, 22–23

Pa'ao, 5
palapala (literacy), 22, 26–27, 35, 39
Pali Highway, 47, 47*f*
pa'u riders, 13*f*, 14
Pi'ilani, 9–10, 12, 14, 18, 46

Pi'ilanihale, 9
pineapple, 61*f*, 65
Pioneer Inn (Pioneer Hotel), 18, 63*f*, 69
Pioneer Mill Company, 50–59, 50*f*, 51*f*, 54*f*, 55*f*, 61*f*, 64–65, 68
Pioneer Mill Hospital, 55*f*
plantation camps, 51, 51*f*, 56, 61, 66
Pōhaku Hauola, 9
poi, 4, 4*f*
Polynesian arrival in Hawai'i, 6
Po'okela Program, 72
potatoes, 6, 8, 10, 42
Puamana, 57-59
Pukui, Mary Kawena, 4
Pu'u Keka'a (Black Rock), 8, 66–67, 66*f*, 67*f*, 69
Pu'u Pa'upa'u, 31

Richards, Clarissa, 18, 23–24, 26
Richards, William, 18, 23–24, 26, 31, 35–36, 35*f*
Royal Kā'anapali Golf Course, 70
Royal Lāhainā Resort, 66, 69

Sandalwood (*'iliahi*), 16, 42
Seamen's Hospital, 44*f*, 64
Shaler, William, 13
Sharpe, Emma Farden, 58–59, 58*f*
Sheraton Maui, 66*f*, 67*f*, 69
Smith, William Owen, 48
Spaulding, Ephriam, 24
Stewart, Charles, 18, 23, 26–27
Stewart, Harriet, 18, 23, 26–27
Stockton, Betsey, 18, 23, 26–27, 26*f*
sugarcane, 3, 25, 49–62, 50*f*, 64, 66
sweet potatoes, 6, 8, 10, 42

taro. See *kalo*
Ten Commandments, 34
tourism, 63–74
Turton, Henry, 50

'ulu (breadfruit), 3–4, 3*f*, 8

Vancouver, George, 10–11

Waine'e (Waiola) Church, 10, 21, 23–25, 25*f*, 28, 28*f*
wars of 1700s, 11–13
water issues, 59–60
West Maui Sugar Association, 50
whalers and whaling industry, 35, 41–45, 41*f*, 43*f*
Whaling Spree, 70*f*, 72
World War II, 60–62, 60*f*, 61*f*, 62*f*

Young, John, 13–14